LAWS AND LEGISLATION

JURISPRUDENCE OF SUPREME COURT JUSTICE STEVENS

LAWS AND LEGISLATION

Additional books in this series can be found on Nova's website under the Series tab.

Additional E-books in this series can be found on Nova's website under the E-book tab.

LAW, CRIME AND LAW ENFORCEMENT

Additional books in this series can be found on Nova's website under the Series tab.

Additional E-books in this series can be found on Nova's website under the E-book tab.

LAWS AND LEGISLATION

JURISPRUDENCE OF SUPREME COURT JUSTICE STEVENS

HARVEY B. LYMONT
EDITOR

Nova Science Publishers, Inc.
New York

For permission to use material from this book please contact us:
Telephone 631-231-7269; Fax 631-231-8175
Web Site: http://www.novapublishers.com

LIBRARY OF CONGRESS CATALOGING-IN-PUBLICATION DATA

Jurisprudence of Supreme Court Justice Stevens / editors, Harvey B. Lymont.
p. cm.
Includes index.
ISBN 978-1-61761-282-4 (softcover)
1. Stevens, John Paul, 1920- 2. United States. Supreme Court. 3. Constitutional Law--United States--Cases. I. Lymont, Harvey B.
KF8745.S78J87 2010
347.73'26--dc22

2010028628

Published by Nova Science Publishers, Inc. ✦ New York

Contents

PREFACE

This book examines the decisions of retiring Justice John Paul Stevens with regard to: select federalism issues; the constitutionality of congressional term limits and the presidential line item veto; select opinions on intellectual property law; decisions on wartime detentions; death penalty jurisprudence; the jury's role in criminal sentencing; the Chevron doctrine; and the Free Speech Clause of the First Amendment.

Chapter 1- Structurally, the Constitution establishes a federal government with discrete, limited powers, reserving authority not given to the federal government under the Constitution to the states and the people. The uncertain contours of this dual system have often resulted in Supreme Court decisions on the reach of the federal government's limited powers and the core autonomy of the states. Congress, for example, has invoked the Commerce Clause to regulate local, and sometimes non-economic, activities that historically have been subject to regulation under state police powers. Also, Congress has invoked its power to enforce the Fourteenth Amendment to regulate state activity that might otherwise be beyond its reach. States, on the other hand, have cited the Tenth Amendment to resist what they perceive as congressional overreaching into essential state functions.

Chapter 2- Justice John Paul Stevens authored the majority opinions in both *U.S. Term Limits, Inc. v. Thornton* and *Clinton v. City of New York*, which struck down term limits for federal legislators and the federal Line Item Veto Act, respectively. While the Supreme Court seems unlikely to address the constitutionality of term limits or the line-item veto in the future, Justice Stevens's conclusion that the absence of constitutional provisions expressly authorizing the exercise of certain powers constitutes a denial of these powers seems likely to influence the Court in the future, particularly in cases involving what Justice Kennedy and others have characterized as "horizontal" or "vertical" separation of powers. Horizontal separation of powers questions involve the relationship between the three branches of the federal government (i.e., legislative, executive, judicial), while vertical separation of powers questions involve the relationship between the federal government, state governments, and individual citizens. In *Term Limits*, the majority held that states lack the power to impose term limits on Members of Congress because the Constitution grants them no such power. Similarly, in *Clinton*, the majority held that a federal statute allowing the President to "cancel" certain provisions of law was unconstitutional because "[t]here is no provision in the Constitution that authorizes the President" to do so. Under these precedents, it would appear that a constitutional amendment would be necessary to allow for either congressional term limits or the presidential line-item veto.

Chapter 3- This chapter briefly surveys decisions of retiring Justice John Paul Stevens in intellectual property cases. An examination of Justice Stevens' written opinions relating to intellectual property law reveals a strong desire to ensure that the rights of intellectual property creators are balanced with the rights of the public to access creative and innovative works. No decision embodies this interest more than Justice Stevens' majority opinion in *Sony Corporation of America v. Universal City Studios, Inc.*, a landmark copyright case issued in 1984 that paved the way for the development and sale of popular consumer electronics, such as the video recorder (VCR, DVR, TiVo), portable music and video players (iPod), personal computers, and other devices that permit the recording and playback of copyrighted content.

In addition, Justice Stevens issued a lengthy dissent in the 2003 case *Eldred v. Ashcroft*, in which he asserted that Congress lacked the power to pass a law that extended the term of existing copyrights by 20 years. Such a retroactive extension delays the entrance of copyrighted works into the public domain and, in Justice Stevens' opinion, is a violation of the Constitution's Copyright Clause that authorizes Congress to grant exclusive intellectual property rights to authors and artists for "limited Times."

Chapter 4- Justice John Paul Stevens played a pivotal role in determining the scope of executive-branch power in a post-9/11 world. After 9/11, Congress quickly authorized the Executive to respond to the terrorist attacks using military force. Difficult legal questions emerged from the consequences of the ensuing military actions, particularly as suspected members of Al Qaeda and the Taliban were captured in Afghanistan and elsewhere and transferred to the U.S. Naval Station at Guantanamo Bay, Cuba. Key questions included: What legal authorities restrict the Executive's ability to detain and try such persons as it sees fit? To what extent do detainees outside of the United States have the right to challenge their detentions in federal courts? When may Congress remove federal courts' jurisdiction over habeas cases?

Justice Stevens authored majority opinions in two leading cases, *Rasul v. Bush* and *Hamdan v. Rumsfeld*, in which the Court allowed detainees' habeas petitions to proceed and invalidated the early incarnation of military commissions, thereby rejecting the broader views of executive power articulated shortly after the 9/11 attacks. In the cases, his view prevailed over strongly articulated dissenting opinions authored by Justice Scalia and other justices.

For a more in-depth examination of the Supreme Court's post-9/11 decisions regarding habeas corpus, see CRS Report RL33180, *Enemy Combatant Detainees: Habeas Corpus Challenges in Federal Court*, by Jennifer K. Elsea and Michael John Garcia.

Chapter 5- Justice Stevens's position on the death penalty has undergone a thorough transformation during his tenure on the Court. Although Stevens initially supported the imposition of the death penalty in accordance with adequately protective state enacted guidelines, over the next 35 years the Justice has voted to narrow the application of the death penalty as he has become more skeptical of the punishment's underlying rationale and the states' ability to protect the rights of capital defendants. In 2008, Justice Stevens's death penalty jurisprudence may have culminated with his concurring opinion in *Baze v. Rees*, in which the Justice unequivocally expressed his ultimate conclusion that the death penalty is itself unconstitutional.

Justice Stevens's position on the death penalty has transformed during his tenure on the Court. Although Stevens initially supported the imposition of the death penalty in accordance with adequately protective state enacted guidelines, over the next 35 years the Justice has voted to narrow the application of the death penalty as he has become more skeptical of the punishment's underlying rationale and the states' ability to protect the rights of capital defendants. In 2008, Justice Stevens questioned the continuing constitutionality of the death penalty in his concurring opinion in *Baze v. Rees*.[1]

Chapter 6- Justice Stevens has played a critical role in the Supreme Court's interpretation of a jury's role in criminal sentencing. In 2000, he wrote the majority opinion for the Court in *Apprendi v. New Jersey*, a landmark case in which the Court held that a judge typically may not increase a sentence beyond the range prescribed by statute unless the increase is based on facts determined by a jury "beyond a reasonable doubt." In 2005, he wrote one of two majority opinions in *United States v. Booker*, in which the Court applied the *Apprendi* rule to the Federal Sentencing Guidelines. In those two cases and in several other cases on this issue during the past few decades, Justice Stevens has been a leading voice, articulating a broad interpretation of the jury trial and due process rights at issue.

Chapter 7- One of Justice John Paul Stevens's most lasting jurisprudential legacies is his opinion in *Chevron v. Natural Resources Defense Council.* The 1984 case, a landmark decision in both administrative law and separation of powers, established the legal framework that has largely governed the degree of deference a court will accord a federal agency in interpreting and implementing statutes. What began as an unexceptional case focusing on the meaning of the phrase "stationary source" in the Clean Air Act has developed into one of the most frequently cited cases ever. Although often relied on as an authority, the case has also engendered significant confusion. Questions of when, and how, to apply the two-step *Chevron* analysis laid out by Justice Stevens, which is simple in theory yet remarkably varied in its application, have consistently challenged federal judges. Moreover, although Justice Stevens has spent the last quarter century working to clarify the *Chevron* doctrine, as he departs the Court he may find himself outside the majority position on at least one key aspect of the test's application.

Chapter 8- Justice Stevens has authored a number of significant opinions expounding upon the constitutional right to freedom of speech. Among them are significant cases related to indecency and the rights of broadcasters ("Seven Dirty Words Case"), commercial speech, symbolic speech, and the freedom of association. This chapter will describe these cases with a view to their impact on free speech case law, and their continuing relevance in the future. This chapter will not discuss Justice Stevens's election law-related opinions

In: Jurisprudence of Supreme Court Justice... ISBN: 978-1-61761-282-4
Editor: Harvey B. Lymont

Chapter 1

THE JURISPRUDENCE OF JUSTICE JOHN PAUL STEVENS: SELECTED FEDERALISM ISSUES

Kenneth R. Thomas

SUMMARY

Structurally, the Constitution establishes a federal government with discrete, limited powers, reserving authority not given to the federal government under the Constitution to the states and the people. The uncertain contours of this dual system have often resulted in Supreme Court decisions on the reach of the federal government's limited powers and the core autonomy of the states. Congress, for example, has invoked the Commerce Clause to regulate local, and sometimes non-economic, activities that historically have been subject to regulation under state police powers. Also, Congress has invoked its power to enforce the Fourteenth Amendment to regulate state activity that might otherwise be beyond its reach. States, on the other hand, have cited the Tenth Amendment to resist what they perceive as congressional overreaching into essential state functions.

During Justice John Paul Stevens's tenure on the Supreme Court, the Court has continued to develop its jurisprudence on these constitutional provisions in resolving tension between federal versus state authority. Justice Stevens himself has written notable opinions on a range of federalism issues.

These opinions generally indicate a viewpoint that it is difficult to clearly distinguish between federal and state spheres of power, and a tendency to recognize a limited federal role in issues that affect state prerogatives and local activities.

Structurally, the Constitution establishes a federal government with discrete, limited powers, Sreserving authority not given to the federal government under the Constitution to the states and the people. However, political and legal notions of the limits of federal power and the core of state autonomy change. As congressional assertions of authority have grown, the Supreme Court has had cause to delimit the reach of federal power in several legal contexts. Frequently contested provisions implicating federal versus state power include the Commerce Clause, the Tenth Amendment, and the Fourteenth Amendment. Justice John Paul Stevens has written notable opinions addressing each of these areas. These opinions generally indicate a viewpoint that it is difficult to clearly distinguish between federal and state spheres of power, and a tendency to recognize a limited federal role in issues that affect state prerogatives and local activities.

THE COMMERCE CLAUSE

The U.S. Constitution provides that Congress shall have the power to regulate commerce with foreign nations and among the various states.[1] Starting in 1937 with the decision in *NLRB v. Jones & Laughlin Steel Corporation*,[2] the Supreme Court took a significant doctrinal step in holding that Congress has the ability to protect interstate commerce from burdens and obstructions that "affect" commerce. In the *NLRB* case, the Court upheld the National Labor Relations Act, finding that control of industrial labor strife was a permissible means of preventing burdens on interstate commerce.[3] Thus, the Court rejected previous distinctions between the economic activities (such as manufacturing) that led up to interstate economic transactions, and the interstate transactions themselves. By allowing Congress to regulate activities that were in the "stream" of commerce, the Court also set the stage for the regulation of a variety of other activities that "affect" commerce. Under this reasoning, the Court upheld many diverse laws, including laws regulating production of wheat on farms,[4] racial discrimination by businesses,[5] and loan-sharking.[6]

In *United States v. Lopez*,[7] however, the Supreme Court brought into question how far Congress can rely on the Commerce Clause as a basis for federal jurisdiction. Under the Gun-Free School Zones Act of 1990, Congress made it a federal offense for "any individual knowingly to possess a firearm at a place that the individual knows, or has reasonable cause to believe, is a school zone."[8] In *Lopez*, the Court held that, because the act neither regulated a commercial activity nor contained a requirement that the possession was connected to interstate commerce, the act exceeded the authority of Congress under the Commerce Clause. Although the Court did not explicitly overrule any previous rulings upholding federal statutes passed under the authority of the Commerce Clause, the decision did appear to suggest new limits on Congress's legislative authority.

Justice Stevens, writing for the Court in *Gonzales v. Raich*, made clear the extent to which Congress still retained authority after *Lopez* to govern individual, localized activities so long as they had potential cumulative economic effects on regulated national markets.[9] *Raich* evaluated an "as applied" challenge to the Controlled Substances Act as regards obtaining, manufacturing, or possessing marijuana for medical purposes. The case was brought by two seriously ill residents of California who used marijuana in compliance with the California Compassionate Use Act of 1996.[10] The challenge was based on the argument that the narrow class of activity being engaged in—the intrastate, noncommercial cultivation and possession of cannabis for personal medical purposes as recommended by a patient's physician pursuant to California state law—did not have a substantial impact on commerce, and thus could not be regulated under the Commerce Clause.[11]

In upholding the application of the Controlled Substances Act in the *Raich* case, Justice Stevens relied on the Court's decision in *Wickard v. Filburn*,[12] which held that "even if appellee's activity be local and though it may not be regarded as commerce, it may still, whatever its nature, be reached by Congress if it exerts a substantial economic effect on interstate commerce."[13] The *Wickard* case upheld the application of the Agricultural Adjustment Act of 1938,[14] which was designed to control prices by regulating the volume of wheat moving in interstate commerce. The Court in *Wickard* held that Congress could regulate not only the wheat sold into commerce, but also wheat retained for consumption on a farm.[15] The Court did so on the theory that the while the impact of wheat consumed on the farm on interstate commerce might be trivial, it was significant when combined with wheat from other farmers similarly situated.[16]

Based on *Wickard*, the Court in *Raich* held that Congress could consider the aggregate effect that allowing the production and consumption of marijuana for medical purposes would have on the illegal market for marijuana.[17] Of even greater concern was that diversion of marijuana grown for medicinal purposes for other uses would frustrate the federal interest in eliminating commercial transactions in the interstate market.[18] In both cases, the Court found that the regulation was within Congress's commerce power because Congress had a rational basis to determine that production of a commodity meant for home consumption, be it wheat or marijuana, could have a substantial effect on supply and demand. In addition, because exempting the use of medical marijuana could undercut enforcement of the Controlled Substances Act, the Court found that the application in this case was within Congress's authority to "make all Laws which shall be necessary and proper"[19] to effectuate its powers. As *Wickard* has traditionally been seen as one of the most expansive interpretations of the Commerce Clause, the Court's reliance on that case seemed to limit the possibility that the Commerce Clause would be likely to be subjected to a major retrenchment.

TENTH AMENDMENT

The powers of the federal government, while limited to those enumerated in the Constitution,[20] have been interpreted expansively at times, so as to create a large potential overlap with state authority. For instance, Article I, § 8, cl. 18 provides that "[t]he Congress shall have Power ... To make all Laws which shall be necessary and proper for carrying into Execution the foregoing Powers and all other Powers vested by this Constitution in the Government of the United States, or in any Department or Officer thereof." Early in the history of the Constitution, the Supreme Court characterized how this clause supplemented the powers of Congress.[21]

Recognizing that the Constitution nevertheless does place limits on the powers of the federal government, the Court has found it difficult to articulate clear principles to define these limits. For instance, for a time, the Court discerned it significant that the Tenth Amendment provides that "powers not delegated to the United States by the Constitution, nor prohibited by it to the States, are reserved to the States respectively, or to the people." While this language would appear to represent a clear example of a federalist principle in the Constitution, it has ultimately had only limited impact in defining the reach of federal authority.

Thus, in *National League of Cities v. Usery*,[22] the Court struck down federal wage and price controls on state and local employees as involving the regulation of core state functions.[23] The author of the opinion, then-Justice Rehnquist, wrote that the statute at issue was unconstitutional because it "displaced the states' freedom to structure integral operations in areas of traditional governmental functions."[24] The opinion first suggested there had to be a limiting principle to guide federalism-based restrictions on national power, and that such a limit must be judicially enforceable.[25] Second, Justice Rehnquist opined that an essential part of state sovereignty was flexibility to determine the compensation state employees would be paid and the hours they would work.[26] Third, he argued that federal wage and price controls substantially interfered with state sovereignty by imposing significant new costs that could "force[] relinquishment of important governmental activities" or "displace[] state policies regarding the manner in which they will structure delivery of those governmental services which their citizens require."[27]

Justice Stevens, who had only recently joined the Court, dissented from the holding in *National League of Cities*, arguing that it was difficult to perceive a defining principle within the majority opinion to distinguish between which state regulations were valid and which were not. The Court, by limiting the application of wage and price controls, was holding that the federal government could not interfere with a state's right to "pay a substandard wage to the janitor at the state capitol." Yet, Justice Stevens argued, there were many ways that the janitor could still be regulated:

> The Federal Government may, I believe, require the State to act impartially when it hires or fires the janitor, to withhold taxes from his paycheck, to observe safety regulations when he is performing his job, to forbid him from burning too much soft coal in the capitol furnace, from dumping untreated refuse in an adjacent waterway, from overloading a state-owned garbage truck, or from driving either the truck or the Governor's limousine over 55 miles an hour. Even though these and many other activities of the capitol janitor are activities of the State qua State, I have no doubt that they are subject to federal regulation.[28]

Justice Stevens's concerns proved to be well-founded. After *National League of Cities*, the lower courts struggled for a number of years to define which "core state functions" were not amenable to federal regulation.[29] For instance, lower federal courts found that providing ambulance services, licensing automobile drivers, and operating a municipal airport were immune from government regulation.[30] On the other hand, the courts had found that issuance of industrial development bonds, regulation of traffic on public roads, and regulation of air transportation were subject to federal regulation.[31] This was the state of the law nine years after *National League of Cities* when the Court decided *Garcia v. San Antonio Metropolitan Transit Authority*.[32]

In *Garcia*, Justice Harry Blackmun reversed course and, in an opinion that Justice Stevens joined, overruled *National League of Cities*. The Court picked up the theme that had been introduced by Justice Stevens:

> We find it difficult, if not impossible, to identify an organizing principle that places each of the cases in the first group on one side of a line and each of the cases in the second group on the other side. The constitutional distinction between licensing drivers and regulating traffic, for example, or between operating a highway authority and operating a mental health facility, is elusive at best.[33]

In sum, the Court in *Garcia* seems to have said that most disputes over the effects on state sovereignty of federal commerce power legislation are to be considered political questions, and that the states should look for relief from federal regulation through the political process.[34] This appeared to have ended the Court's attempt to substantively limit federal government regulation of the states.

The Court soon turned, however, to the question of how the Constitution limits the means by which the federal government regulates the states. In *New York v. United States*,[35] Congress had attempted to regulate in the area of low-level radioactive waste. In a 1985 statute, Congress provided that states must either develop legislation on how to dispose of all low-level radioactive waste generated within the state, or the state would be forced to take title to such waste, which would mean that it became the state's responsibility. The Court found that although Congress had the authority under the Commerce Clause to regulate low-level radioactive waste, it only had the power to regulate the waste directly. Here, Congress had attempted to require the states to perform the regulation, and decreed that the failure to do so would require the state to deal with the financial consequences of owning large quantities of radioactive waste. In effect, Congress sought to "commandeer" the legislative process of the states. In the *New York* case, the Court found that this power was not found in the text or structure of the Constitution, and it was thus a violation of the Tenth Amendment.

A later case presented the question of the extent to which Congress could regulate through a state's executive branch officers. This case, *Printz v. United States*,[36] involved the Brady Handgun Act. The Brady Handgun Act required state and local law-enforcement officers to conduct background checks on prospective handgun purchasers within five business days of an attempted purchase. This portion of the act was challenged under the Tenth Amendment, under the theory that Congress was without authority to "commandeer" state executive branch officials. After a historical study of federal commandeering of state officials, the Court concluded that commandeering of state executive branch officials was, like commandeering of the legislature, outside of Congress's power, and consequently a violation of the Tenth Amendment.

Justice Stevens, in dissent, pointed to a practical concern with the Court's Tenth Amendment decisions. By limiting the authority of the federal government to allow states to share in the establishment of federal policy, the Court seemed to invite even more pervasive federal regulation. Hence, the rule actually may encourage the federal government to assume even greater authority. As Justice Stevens argued in *Printz*,

> Perversely, the majority's rule seems more likely to damage than to preserve the safeguards against tyranny provided by the existence of vital state governments. By limiting the ability of the Federal Government to enlist state officials in the implementation of its programs, the Court creates incentives for the National Government to aggrandize itself. In the name of states' rights, the majority would have the Federal Government create vast national bureaucracies to implement its policies. This is exactly the sort of thing that the early Federalists promised would not occur, in part as a result of the National Government's ability to rely on the magistracy of the States.[37]

FOURTEENTH AMENDMENT

Section 5 of the Fourteenth Amendment is a significant, yet circumscribed, source of congressional power. The Fourteenth Amendment provides that states shall not deprive persons of "life, liberty, or property" without due process of law nor deprive them of equal protection of the laws. Section 5 empowers Congress to legislate to enforce the amendment. When Congress has properly acted under § 5, the courts are more deferential toward federal regulation of state action than they might be when Congress exercises other powers. That is, the courts have upheld limits on state autonomy under § 5 that might not otherwise be sustainable under the Constitution.

Interpretations of when Congress may use its § 5 powers, however, have been in flux over the years. At issue has been how expansively Congress may act to "enforce" rights, as opposed to creating or more generally protecting them. For example, in the case of *Flores v. City of Boerne*,[38] the Court struck down the Religious Freedom Restoration Act (RFRA) as beyond the authority of Congress under § 5 of the Fourteenth Amendment. In enacting RFRA, Congress had cited its § 5 powers to require a state to show a compelling state interest before applying an otherwise neutral state law to religion. Congress took this step after the Court had held in *Oregon v. Smith*[39] that the Freedom of Exercise Clause of the First Amendment did not require a state to demonstrate a compelling interest before it could apply a generally applicable drug regulation to peyote use during a religious ceremony.

The *City of Boerne* case arose when the City of Boerne, TX, denied a church a building permit to expand, because the church was in a designated historical district. The church challenged the zoning decision under RFRA. The Supreme Court reiterated that § 5 of the Fourteenth Amendment gave Congress the power to enforce existing constitutional protections, but found that this did not automatically include the power to pass any legislation to protect these rights. Instead, the Court held that there must be a "congruence and proportionality" between the injury to be remedied and the law adopted to that end. Rather than an attempt to remedy a problem, RFRA was seen by the Court as an attempt by Congress to overturn an unpopular Supreme Court decision. The law focused on no one area of alleged harm to religion, but rather just broadly inhibited state and local regulations of all types. Consequently, the Court found RFRA to be an overbroad response to a relatively nonexistent problem.

The "congruence and proportionality" test in *Boerne* for sustaining an exercise of § 5 powers became a formidable hurdle in other contexts as particular regulation of the states was held to be unsustainable under other means. For example, though Congress has broad power to regulate a wide range of activities under the Commerce Clause, the Court has held that Congress cannot authorize suits against states for violations of federal laws enacted under its commerce authority: in such circumstances, state sovereign immunity under the Eleventh Amendment prevails. On the other hand, Congress could abrogate state sovereign immunity when it acted under § 5, but a line of cases applying *Boerne* reiterated that § 5 power was generally circumscribed.

Then, in a 2004 decision written by Justice Stevens, the Court took a different analytical tack in upholding certain suits against states for violating the Americans with Disabilities Act (ADA). In *Tennessee v. Lane*,[40] two paraplegic plaintiffs alleged that the State of Tennessee and several of its counties violated Title II of the ADA, which requires that the disabled be provided access to public services, programs, and activities, by failing to provide physical access to state courts.[41] Analyzing the case as an attempt to ensure a fundamental right to access courts as part of Due Process instead of as an antidiscrimination measure to ensure Equal Protection, the Court held that Title II, as applied to this right of access to the courts, was a proper exercise of Congress's authority under § 5 of the Fourteenth Amendment to abrogate states' Eleventh Amendment immunity.[42]

In applying the *Boerne* congruence and proportionality test, the Court in *Lane* noted that the right protected in Title II of the act was access to public services, programs, and activities. While the unequal treatment of the disabled would only generally be a constitutional violation enforceable under § 5 if it were irrational, the Court emphasized that Title II was also intended to reach the more rigorously protected rights of the Due Process Clause of the Fourteenth Amendment, such as the right of access to the courts.[43] The Court stated that these due process rights required a higher standard of protection than would generally apply. The limited nature of Title II as a remedy for the denial of the right of access to courts also informed the Court's holding that the measure is a valid prophylactic remedy.[44]

End Notes

[1] U.S. Const., Art. I, § 8, cl. 3.
[2] 301 U.S. 1 (1937).
[3] 301 U.S. at 41.
[4] Id.
[5] *See* Heart of Atlanta Motel v. United States, 370 U.S. 241 (1964); Katzenbach v. McClung, 379 U.S. 241 (1964).
[6] Perez v. United States, 402 U.S. 146 (1971).
[7] 514 U.S. 549 (1995).
[8] 18 U.S.C. § 922(q)(1)A).
[9] 125 S. Ct. 2195 (2005).
[10] Cal. Health & Safety Code Ann § 11362.5 (West Supp. 2005) (providing for the legal possession of medical marijuana by a patient or primary care-giver, upon the written or oral recommendation of a physician).
[11] 125 S. Ct. at 2211.
[12] 317 U.S. 111 (1942).
[13] Id. at 125.

[14] 52 Stat. 31.
[15] Id. at 128-29.
[16] Id. at 127.
[17] 125 U.S. at 2207.
[18] Id.
[19] U.S. Const., Art. I, § 8.
[20] Article I, § 1, of the Constitution provides that "All legislative powers herein granted shall be vested in a Congress of the United States." Unlike a typical grant of power to states, Article I, § 1, does not grant to Congress "all legislative power," but rather grants to Congress only those specific powers enumerated in § 8 and elsewhere in the Constitution.
[21] As stated by Chief Justice Marshall in *McCulloch v. Maryland*, 17 U.S. (4 Wheat.) 316 (1819): "Let the end be legitimate, let it be within the scope of the Constitution, and all means which are appropriate, which are plainly adapted to that end, which are not prohibited, but consist with the letter and spirit of the Constitution, are constitutional."
[22] 426 U.S. 833 (1976).
[23] In *National League of Cities v. Usery*, the Court conceded that the legislation under attack, which regulated the wages and hours of certain state and local governmental employees, was undoubtedly within the scope of the Commerce Clause, but it cautioned that there are attributes of sovereignty attaching to every state government which may not be impaired by Congress, not because Congress may lack an affirmative grant of legislative authority to reach the matter, but because the Constitution prohibits it from exercising the authority in that manner.
[24] 426 U.S. at 852.
[25] 426 U.S. at 842.
[26] 426 U.S. at 845.
[27] 426 U.S. at 847.
[28] Id. at 880-81.
[29] In *Hodel v. Virginia Surface Mining & Recl. Assn.*, 452 U.S. 264, 276-277 (1981), the Court summarized the four conditions to establish a core state function. First, the federal statute must regulate "the 'States as States.'" Second, the statute must "address matters that are indisputably '[attributes] of state sovereignty.'" Third, state compliance with the federal obligation must "directly impair [the States'] ability 'to structure integral operations in areas of traditional governmental functions.'" Finally, the relation of state and federal interests must not be such that "the nature of the federal interest ... justifies state submission." 452 U.S. at 287-288, and n. 29, quoting *National League of Cities*, 426 U.S. at 845, 852, 854.
[30] Gold Cross Ambulance v. City of Kansas City, 538 F.Supp. 956, 967-969 (WD Mo. 1982), *aff'd on other grounds*, 705 F.2d 1005 (CA8 1983)(ambulance services); United States v. Best, 573 F.2d 1095, 1102-1103 (CA9 1978)(auto licenses); Amersbach v. City of Cleveland, 598 F.2d 1033, 1037-1038 (CA6 1979)(municipal airport).
[31] Woods v. Homes and Structures of Pittsburg, Kansas, Inc., 489 F.Supp. 1270, 1296-1297 (Kan. 1980)(industrial bonds); Friends of the Earth v. Carey, 552 F.2d 25, 38 (CA2), cert. denied, 434 U.S. 902 (1977)(public roads); Hughes Air Corp. v. Public Utilities Comm'n of Cal., 644 F.2d 1334, 1340-1341 (CA9 1981)(air transportation).
[32] 469 U.S. 528 (1985).
[33] 469 U.S. at 538.
[34] *See also South Carolina v. Baker*, 485 U.S. 505 (1988).
[35] 505 U.S. 144 (1992).
[36] 521 U.S. 898 (1997).
[37] 521 U.S. at 959.
[38] 521 U.S. 507 (1997).
[39] 494 U.S. 872 (1990).
[40] 541 U.S. 509 (2004).

[41] One plaintiff in *Lane* claimed he was unable to appear to answer criminal charges on the second floor of a courthouse that had no elevator. The second plaintiff, a certified court reporter, claimed she was denied the opportunity both to work and to participate in the judicial process because she was unable to access numerous county courthouses.

[42] The Court cited congressional evidence that legislative attempts preceding Title II inadequately addressed the problem of patterned unconstitutional treatment in access to the courts. 541 U.S. at 526.

[43] The Court held that it need not examine Title II as a whole when evaluating the remedy's congruence and proportionality to the injury of disability discrimination in access to the courts. The relevant inquiry solely concerned Title II's scope as applied to the rights associated with access to judicial services. The Court cited as precedent for this limited application approach the *Garrett* case, in which it considered only Title I of the ADA for purposes of Fourteenth Amendment analysis. Based on this narrow scope of inquiry, the Court determined that both the pattern of past discrimination in access to the courts and the failure of previous legislative attempts to remedy the injury were sufficient to hold that Title II is a valid exercise of Congress's power under § 5 of the Fourteenth Amendment.

[44] Title II does not require states to compromise the integrity of public programs or make unduly burdensome changes to public facilities. 541 U.S. at 532. Rather, states need only take reasonable measures to comply with Title II regulations. Id.

In: Jurisprudence of Supreme Court Justice... ISBN: 978-1-61761-282-4
Editor: Harvey B. Lymont

Chapter 2

The Jurisprudence of Justice John Paul Stevens: The Constitutionality of Congressional Term Limits and the Presidential Line Item Veto

Kate M. Manuel

Summary

Justice John Paul Stevens authored the majority opinions in both *U.S. Term Limits, Inc. v. Thornton* and *Clinton v. City of New York*, which struck down term limits for federal legislators and the federal Line Item Veto Act, respectively. While the Supreme Court seems unlikely to address the constitutionality of term limits or the line-item veto in the future, Justice Stevens's conclusion that the absence of constitutional provisions expressly authorizing the exercise of certain powers constitutes a denial of these powers seems likely to influence the Court in the future, particularly in cases involving what Justice Kennedy and others have characterized as "horizontal" or "vertical" separation of powers. Horizontal separation of powers questions involve the relationship between the three branches of the federal government (i.e., legislative, executive, judicial), while vertical separation of powers questions involve the relationship between the federal government, state governments, and individual citizens. In *Term Limits*, the majority held that states lack the power to impose term limits on Members of Congress because the Constitution grants them no such power. Similarly, in *Clinton*, the majority held that a federal statute allowing the President to "cancel" certain provisions of law was unconstitutional because "[t]here is no provision in the Constitution that authorizes the President" to do so. Under these precedents, it would appear that a constitutional amendment would be necessary to allow for either congressional term limits or the presidential line-item veto.

The opinions authored by Justice Stevens in *Term Limits* and *Clinton* are consistent with what commentators have characterized as his generally "pro federalist" approach to other issues, such as those involving the Commerce Clause, the Tenth Amendment, and the Fourteenth Amendment. For a more in-depth discussion of his approach to federalism, see CRS Report R41244, *The Jurisprudence of Justice John Paul Stevens: Selected Federalism Issues*, by Kenneth R. Thomas.

INTRODUCTION

Justice John Paul Stevens authored the majority opinions in both *U.S. Term Limits, Inc. v. Thornton* and *Clinton v. City of New York*, which struck down term limits for federal legislators and the federal Line Item Veto Act, respectively.[1] While the Supreme Court seems unlikely to address the constitutionality of term limits or the line-item veto in the future,[2] Justice Stevens's conclusion that the absence of constitutional provisions expressly authorizing the exercise of certain powers constitutes a denial of these powers seems likely to influence the Court in the future, particularly in cases involving what Justice Kennedy and others have characterized as "horizontal" or "vertical" separation of powers.[3] Horizontal separation of powers questions involve the relationship between the three branches of the federal government (i.e., legislative, executive, judicial), while vertical separation of powers questions involve the relationship between the federal government, state governments, and individual citizens.[4] In *Term Limits*, the majority held that states lack the power to impose term limits on Members of Congress because the Constitution grants them no such power.[5] Similarly, in *Clinton*, the majority held that a federal statute allowing the President to "cancel" certain provisions of law was unconstitutional because "[t]here is no provision in the Constitution that authorizes the President" to do so.[6] Under these precedents, it would appear that a constitutional amendment would be necessary to allow for either congressional term limits or the presidential line-item veto.[7]

U.S. TERM LIMITS, INC. V. THORNTON

"Term limits," or legal restrictions upon the number of terms that an individual may serve in an elected office, became a matter of significant public interest in the early 1990s, in part because of allegations that incumbents become less responsive to their constituents as they become more "entrenched."[8] Between 1990 and 1994, 23 states imposed term limits on elected officials,[9] and by 1995, over 40% of the Members of Congress were ostensibly term limited.[10] One of the states to enact term limits was Arkansas. On November 3, 1992, Arkansas voters adopted a ballot initiative amending the state constitution to impose term limits on members of the Arkansas legislature and prohibit the inclusion on the general election ballot of the names of otherwise-eligible candidates for the U.S. House of Representatives or Senate who had served a specified number of terms.[11] A state trial court found that the provisions concerning the inclusion of incumbents on ballots were unconstitutional because they violated the Qualifications Clauses of the U.S. Constitution.[12] The Arkansas Supreme Court affirmed,[13] prompting the appeal to the U.S. Supreme Court that gave rise to Justice Stevens's opinion for the majority in *U.S. Term Limits*.

Qualifications Clauses and *Powell v. McCormack*

Term Limits was the first case since *Powell v. McCormack*, which was decided six years before Justice Stevens joined the Court, to address the Qualifications Clauses of the U.S. Constitution. These clauses provide that

> No Person shall be a Representative who shall not have attained to the Age of twenty five Years, and been seven Years a Citizen of the United States, and who shall not, when elected, be an Inhabitant of that State in which he shall be chosen. ...
>
> No Person shall be a Senator who shall not have attained to the Age of thirty Years, and been nine Years a Citizen of the United States, and who shall not, when elected, be an Inhabitant of that State for which he shall be chosen.[14]

The *Powell* Court had relied upon historical evidence, including debates regarding qualifications for federal legislators at the constitutional convention, and "an examination of the basic principles of our democratic system" to find that Congress lacked the power to impose additional qualifications upon its Members.[15] However, the decision in *Powell* did not address whether states could impose additional qualifications upon Members, something that some commentators asserted was within states' "reserved powers" under the Tenth Amendment.[16] The Tenth Amendment provides that "[t]he powers not delegated to the United States by the Constitution, nor prohibited by it to the States, are reserved to the States respectively, or to the people."[17]

Justice Stevens's Opinion for the Majority

In *Term Limits*, Justice Stevens, writing for a majority of the Court, found that states also lack the power to impose additional qualifications upon Members of Congress.[18] After reaffirming *Powell*, which he acknowledged was not dispositive,[19] Justice Stevens concluded that the power to add qualifications could not have been reserved to the states by the Tenth Amendment because it did not exist prior to the ratification of the Constitution, which created Congress, and so was not within the "original powers" of the states.[20] Alternatively, he concluded that even if the states had possessed some original power to set Representatives' qualifications, the "Framers intended the Constitution to be the exclusive source of qualifications for Members of Congress, and that the Framers thereby 'divested' States of any power to add qualifications."[21]

In so concluding, Justice Stevens relied on the text of the Constitution, which expressly delegates certain powers related to federal elections to the states (e.g., determining the time, place, and manner of federal elections);[22] the Framers' intent, as evidenced by the convention and ratification debates;[23] the post-ratification practice of the states;[24] and "democratic principles," including the potential effect of allowing states to formulate diverse qualifications upon the "egalitarian ideal" embodied in the Constitution.[25] Justice Stevens also relied heavily on the precedent of *McCulloch v. Maryland*, an 1819 decision that noted that states cannot "surrender" powers they never had,[26] and *Garcia v. San Antonio Metropolitan Transit Authority*, a 1985 case holding that states retain sovereign authority "only to the extent that the Constitution has not divested them of their original powers and transferred those powers to the Federal Government."[27] Justice Stevens had joined with the majority in

Garcia, rejecting the argument that the powers reserved to the states by the Tenth Amendment impose certain affirmative limits upon Congress's exercise of its enumerated powers.[28]

Justice Thomas's Dissenting Opinion

It is in treating constitutional "silence"—or the lack of provisions expressly authorizing states to impose additional qualifications on Members of Congress—as a denial of that power that Justice Stevens's opinion for the majority arguably diverges most markedly from Justice Thomas's dissenting opinion. Justice Thomas would, in contrast, treat "silence"—or the lack of provisions expressly prohibiting states from imposing additional qualifications—as proof that the states possess that power:

> The Federal Government and the States ... face different default rules: Where the Constitution is silent about the exercise of a particular power—that is, where the Constitution does not speak either expressly or by necessary implication—the Federal Government lacks that power and the States enjoy it.[29]

This difference, in turn, reflects markedly different views of the breadth of states' reserved powers under the Tenth Amendment, as well as markedly different approaches to what Justice Kennedy and other commentators have characterized as "vertical" separation of powers.[30] While Justice Thomas would construe the range of powers reserved to the states broadly in order to protect individuals from the federal government,[31] Justice Stevens would construe the range of powers reserved to the states narrowly in order to protect the federal government from the states.[32]

CLINTON V. CITY OF NEW YORK

Writing for the majority in *Clinton v. City of New York*, Justice Stevens relied upon a similar approach to "silence," or the absence of constitutional provisions authorizing the President to amend or repeal statutes, in striking down the federal Line Item Veto Act of 1996.[33] Much like term limits, the line-item veto attracted significant popular attention in the 1990s because of concerns about alleged shortcomings in the democratic process, most notably "the persistent practice by Congress of attaching riders and other nongermane amendments to legislation as a means to impel enactment and avoid a veto."[34] The Line Item Veto Act authorized the President to "cancel in whole ... (1) any dollar amount of discretionary budget authority; (2) any item of new direct spending; or (3) any limited tax benefit" after considering the legislative history of the provisions and making certain determinations.[35] Some Members of Congress, among others, challenged the statute shortly after its enactment, but were found to lack standing because they had not alleged a "sufficiently concrete injury."[36] Justice Stevens dissented here and would have recognized Members' standing because "deprivation" of the "right to vote on the precise text that will ultimately become law" constitutes a sufficient injury "to provide every Member of Congress with standing to challenge the constitutionality of the statute."[37] Shortly thereafter, however, President Clinton exercised his authority under the act to cancel an item of new direct spending and a limited tax benefit, thereby giving rise to the litigation in *Clinton*.[38] Standing remained an issue in *Clinton*,[39] and Justice Stevens's opinion for the majority is cited more for its treatment of standing than for anything else.[40]

Justice Stevens's Opinion for the Majority

Having found that the plaintiffs have standing, Justice Stevens, writing for the majority, proceeded to find the federal line-item veto unconstitutional because "[t]here is no provision in the Constitution that authorizes the President to enact, to amend, or to repeal statutes."[41] In reaching this conclusion, Justice Stevens focused upon the Bicameralism and Presentment Clauses of the U.S. Constitution (Article I, Section 7, Clauses 2 & 3), which authorize Presidents to "return" bills that they disapprove of to Congress before they become law, but otherwise do not provide for Presidents to amend bills that have been enacted.[42] He further noted that the historical materials support the conclusion that the failure of the Bicameralism and Presentment Clauses to provide for presidential "repeal" of statutes meant that the President could not exercise this power.[43]

Justice Stevens also relied upon *INS v. Chadha*, a 1983 decision which held that "[r]epeal of statutes, no less than enactment, must conform with [Article] I."[44] Justice Stevens had joined with the majority in *Chadha*, striking down legislation that allowed Congress to exercise the "legislative veto," or revoke certain executive branch decisions without enacting legislation (i.e., with the vote of a chamber or committee). Because he viewed cancellation of certain provisions of enacted statutes as tantamount to their repeal, he found *Chadha* dispositive.[45] Justice Stevens further found that the present case was distinguishable from *Field v. Clark*, an 1892 decision upholding the constitutionality of the Tariff Act of 1890, because the Tariff Act authorized the President to decline to spend funds appropriated under the act, while the Line Item Veto Act authorized the President to "cancel" certain provisions of other enacted statutes.[46]

Dissenting Opinions by Justice Breyer and Justice Scalia

Justice Stevens declined to reach the separation of powers argument that formed one basis for the lower court's decision striking down the line-item veto[47] and played a prominent role in the two dissenting opinions. Justice Breyer, in contrast, found that the act did not violate "Separation of Powers principles" and constituted a proper delegation of legislative power to the President,[48] while Justice Scalia reached similar conclusions on somewhat different grounds.[49] The separation of powers concerns here were "horizontal ones," focused on "maintain[ing] the tripartite structure of the Federal government ... by providing a 'safeguard against the encroachment or aggrandizement of one branch at the expense of the other.'"[50] While Courts have struck down certain "encroachments" by one branch upon the powers of another,[51] they have also permitted Congress, in particular, to delegate some of its legislative power to other branches provided the delegation is "under the limitation of a prescribed standard."[52]

However, although he did not reach the issue, Justice Stevens's approach may suggest that certain delegations are impermissible unless expressly authorized in the Constitution, or even that certain manifestations of the separation of powers provided for in the Constitution are unalterable without a constitutional amendment. While he acknowledged that the Line Item Veto Act authorized the President to "effect the repeal of laws," Justice Stevens nonetheless stated,

> The fact that Congress intended such a result is of no moment. Although Congress presumably anticipated that the President might cancel some of the items in the Balanced Budget Act and in the Taxpayer Relief Act, Congress cannot alter the procedures set out in Article I, § 7, without amending the Constitution.[53]

JUSTICE STEVENS'S LEGACY

Justice Stevens's treatment of constitutional "silence" in separation of powers cases arguably constitutes one of his legacies,[54] in part, because the majority opinion in *Term Limits* came after the Court's decision in *United States v. Lopez* and can be seen as limiting the "antifederalist revival" that some commentators saw occurring with *Lopez* and the *Term Limits* dissent.[55] In *Lopez*, a majority struck down a federal law that prohibited the possession of guns within 1,000 feet of a school, in part, on the grounds that the absence of limits on federal power would unacceptably obliterate the "distinction between what is truly national and what is truly local."[56] The *Term Limits* dissent took a similar approach to federal power, asserting that the federal government may exercise only those powers enumerated in the Constitution, while state governments may exercise all powers not denied to them in the Constitution or elsewhere (e.g., state constitutions).[57]

Although the *Lopez* majority opinion and the *Term Limits* dissent were generally read at the time as portending a possible resurgence of Tenth Amendment-based or other limitations on federal power,[58] this resurgence arguably has not extended beyond the Court's Commerce Clause jurisprudence, at least to date. Some cases, most notably *United States v. Morrison*, later found the enactment of particular federal statutes exceeded Congress's Commerce powers.[59] The Tenth Amendment, in contrast, has arguably remained "dormant" as a source of substantive limitations on federal power, notwithstanding the *Term Limits* dissent.[60] Justice Stevens also played a significant role in other cases taking what commentators have characterized as a generally "pro federalist" approach to interpreting the Commerce Clause, the Tenth Amendment, and the Fourteenth Amendment. For a more in-depth discussion of his approach to federalism, see CRS Report R41244, *The Jurisprudence of Justice John Paul Stevens: Selected Federalism Issues*, by Kenneth R. Thomas.

Justice Stevens's opinion in *Clinton* arguably expanded on the treatment of constitutional "silence" in *Term Limits*, suggesting that, at least in certain cases, lack of constitutional provisions authorizing the exercise of particular powers precludes delegation of these powers to another branch of the federal government, notwithstanding the consent of the branch delegating the power.[61]

End Notes

[1] Clinton v. City of New York, 524 U.S. 417 (1998); U.S. Term Limits, Inc. v. Thornton, 514 U.S. 779 (1995). Term limits for state legislators and state line item veto statutes were not at issue in these cases, but have generally been upheld. *See, e.g.*, Ray v. Mortham, 742 So. 2d 1276 (Fla. 1999) (upholding term limits for state legislators); Rush v. Ray, 362 N.W.2d 479 (Iowa 1985) (upholding, but limiting, the line item veto authority of the governor of Iowa).

[2] *Cf.* Stanley H. Friedelbaum, *Term Limits, the State Courts, and National Dominion: The Vicissitudes of American Federalism*, 60 ALB. L. REV. 1567, 1580 (1997) ("It is unlikely that any further cases concerning term limits in any form will be considered by the United States Supreme Court.").

[3] *Clinton*, 524 U.S. at 452 (Kennedy, J., concurring) ("Separation of powers helps to ensure the ability of each branch to be vigorous in asserting its proper authority. In this respect the device operates on a horizontal axis to secure a proper balance of legislative, executive, and judicial authority. Separation of powers operates on a vertical axis as well, between each branch and the citizens in whose interest powers must be exercised."); Kathleen M. Sullivan, *Dueling Sovereignties*: U.S. Term Limits, Inc. v. Thornton, 109 HARV. L. REV. 78, 91-92 (1995) (noting parallels between horizontal and vertical separation of powers cases).

[4] Approaches to vertical separation of powers cases can differ as to whether, and to what degree, the states play a role in checking the power of the federal government vis-à-vis individual citizens. Justice Stevens's approach arguably would not accord states a significant role here, while Justice Thomas's approach would. *Compare Term Limits*, 514 U.S. at 837-38 (rejecting the notion that Members of Congress represent individuals through the states) *with* 514 U.S. at 859 ("[W]hile the majority is correct that the Framers expected the selection process to create a 'direct link' between Members of the House of Representatives and the people, ... the link was between the Representatives from each State and the people of that State.").

[5] *Id.* at 800 ("Petitioners argue that the Constitution contains no express prohibition against state-added qualifications, and that [Arkansas's term limit amendment] is therefore an appropriate exercise of a State's reserved power to place additional restrictions on the choices that its own voters may make. We disagree ...").

[6] *Clinton*, 524 U.S. at 438. *See also id.* at 439 ("There are powerful reasons for construing constitutional silence on this profoundly important issue as equivalent to an express prohibition.").

[7] Resolutions to amend the Constitution to allow for the presidential line item veto have been introduced in the 111th Congress (H.J.Res. 15, S.J.Res. 22). Additional bills referencing the "line item veto" in their titles have also been introduced (e.g., H.R. 1294, S. 524), but would not allow the President to "cancel" provisions of federal law in the same manner as the Line Item Veto Act of 1996. Rather, under these bills, the President would propose the repeal of "congressional earmarks" or the cancellation of "limited tariff benefits" or "targeted tax benefits," and Congress would give "expedited consideration" to legislation enacting these proposals.

[8] *See, e.g.*, *Term Limits*, 514 U.S. at 784 (quoting the preamble to the Arkansas term limit amendment, which stated, "The people of Arkansas find and declare that elected officials who remain in office too long become preoccupied with reelection and ignore their duties as representatives of the people. Entrenched incumbency has reduced voter participation and has led to an electoral system that is less free, less competitive, and less representative.").

[9] David G. Savage, *High Court Bars States from Limiting Congressional Terms*, L.A. TIMES, May 23, 1995, at A1.

[10] Kris W. Kobach, Note, *Rethinking Article V: Term Limits and the Seventeenth and Nineteenth Amendments*, 103 YALE L. J. 1971, 1971 (1994).

[11] *Term Limits*, 514 U.S. at 784. Writing for the majority, Justice Stevens found that this ostensible ballot-access restriction constituted a de facto term limit because it represented "an indirect attempt to accomplish what the Constitution prohibits Arkansas from accomplishing directly." 514 U.S. at 829 (internal quotations omitted). The dissent disagreed, noting that the challenged provisions would not bar incumbents from serving provided they were elected by write-in votes. 514 U.S. at 918 (Thomas, J., dissenting). The attempt to characterize the Arkansas amendments as a ballot access provision was significant because the Constitution expressly grants states the power to regulate the "Times, Places, and Manner of holding Elections." U.S. Const. art. I, § 4, cl. 1.

[12] U.S. Term Limits, Inc. v. Hill, 872 S.W.2d 349, 353 (Ark. 1994).

[13] *Id.* at 365.

[14] U.S. Const. art. I, § 2, cl. 2 (qualifications of Representatives); art. I, § 3, cl. 3 (qualifications of Senators).

[15] 395 U.S. 486, 541-48 (1969). In *Powell*, the Court found that Adam Clayton Powell, Jr., of New York had been unconstitutionally excluded from membership in the House after a House committee determined that he had wrongfully diverted House funds for personal use and made false reports regarding expenditures. 395 U.S. at 489-93.

[16] *See, e.g.*, Joyner v. Mofford, 706 F.2d 1523, 1528 (9th Cir. 1983) ("In *Powell* …, the Supreme Court accepted this restrictive view of the Qualifications Clause—*at least as applied to Congress*.") (emphasis added); Stumpf v. Lau, 839 P.3d 120, 129 (Nev. 1992) (Steffen, J., dissenting) (noting the possible reservation to the people of the right to enact "state constitutional provisions adding reasonable qualifications beyond those specified in the qualifications clauses").

[17] U.S. Const. amend. X.

[18] *Term Limits*, 514 U.S. at 837.

[19] *Id.* at 798 ("Our reaffirmation of *Powell* does not necessarily resolve the specific questions presented.").

[20] *Id.* at 802 (relying on Justice Story's conclusion that "the states can exercise no powers whatsoever, which exclusively spring out of the existence of the national government, which the constitution does not delegate to them. … No state can say, that is has reserved, what it never possessed.").

[21] *Id.* at 800-01.

[22] *Id.* at 804-05. Justice Stevens noted that the Constitution also expressly delegates to states the power to "appoint, in such Manner as the Legislature … may direct, a Number of Electors." *Id.* at 805. He contrasted these express delegations of power with the express limitations on states' power vis-à-vis the federal legislature. *Id.* at 804 (noting that the Constitution gives Congress the "final say" in determining the qualifications of the representatives of the various states and requires that Members' salaries be set by statute and paid from the U.S. Treasury).

[23] *Id.* at 806-15. *See especially id.* at 805 ("[T]he Qualifications Clauses were intended to preclude the States from exercising any such power and to fix as exclusive the qualifications in the Constitution.").

[24] *Id.* at 815-19 (noting that Congress first considered a challenge to a Member's qualifications in 1807 and its resolution of this challenge was subsequently construed to mean that states lacked the power to impose qualifications. The 1807 challenge involved William McCreery, a Representative from Maryland, who allegedly did not satisfy the state's residency requirement. Congress resolved the challenge by finding that he met the putative state qualifications.

[25] *Id.* at 819-22.

[26] *Id.* at 802 (quoting 17 U.S. 316, 430 (1819)). Justice Stevens construed *McCulloch* as rejecting "the argument that the Constitution's silence on the subject of state power to tax corporations chartered by Congress implies that the States have 'reserved' power to tax such federal instrumentalities.").

[27] *Id.* at 801 (quoting *Garcia v. San Antonio Metropolitan Transit Authority*, 469 U.S. 528, 549 (1985)).

[28] 469 U.S. 528, 552 (1985) (upholding application of a federal law setting maximum hours and minimum wages to state and local government employees, in part, on the grounds that the states' role in the selection of the executive and legislative branches of the federal government means that there is no need to fashion any discrete limitations on the objects of federal authority vis-à-vis "traditional state government functions"), *rev'g* Nat'l League of Cities v. Usery, 426 U.S. 833 (1976) (finding that application of a federal law setting maximum hours and minimum wages to state and local government employees violated an "affirmative structural immunity" of the states). In contrast, Justice Thomas, writing for the dissent, distinguished *Garcia* from *Term Limits* on the grounds that "*Garcia* dealt with an entirely different issue: the extent to which principles of state sovereignty implicit in our federal system curtail Congress' authority to exercise its enumerated powers. ... The question raised by the present case, however, is not whether any principle of state sovereignty implicit in the Tenth Amendment bars congressional action that Article I appears to authorize, but rather whether Article I bars state action that it does not appear to forbid." *Term Limits*, 514 U.S. at 852-53.

[29] *Term Limits*, 514 U.S. at 848 (Thomas, J., dissenting).

[30] *See supra* notes 3 and 4.

[31] *Term Limits*, 514 U.S. at 857 ("In a range of cases concerning the federal/state relation, ... this Court has deemed positions taken in Story's commentaries to be more nationalist than the Constitution warrants."); *id.* at 868 ("Even if one were willing to ignore the distinction between requirements enshrined in the Constitution and other requirements that the Framers were content to leave within the reach of ordinary law, Story's application of the *expressio unius* maxim takes no account of federalism."). The references to "Story" here are to Justice Story, whose commentaries the majority quoted in several places, including the passage cited, *supra*, in note 20.

[32] *See, e.g.*, *Term Limits*, 514 U.S. at 808 ("The Framers feared that the diverse interests of the States would undermine the National Legislature."); *id.* at 811 ("Given the Framers' wariness over the potential for state abuse ..."); *id.* at 822 ("Permitting individual States to formulate diverse qualifications for their representatives would ... undermin[e] the uniformity and the national character that the Framers envisioned and sought to ensure."). *See also id.* at 842 (Kennedy, J., concurring) "Nothing in the Constitution or The Federalist Papers ... supports the idea of state interference with the most basic relation between the National Government and its citizens."). Several commentators have noted Justice Stevens's reliance on the "organic theory of the Union," rooted in *McCulloch*, and concomitant concerns regarding state interference in national concerns. *See, e.g.*, Friedelbaum, *supra* note 2, at 1578; Robert F. Nagel, *The Term Limits Dissent: What Nerve*, 38 ARIZ. L. REV. 843, 844, 849 (1996) (construing the majority opinion as "battl[ing] with the notion that this nation is merely 'a collection of states'"); Sullivan, *supra* note 3, at 110 ("The Court thus replayed the role it had first fashioned in *McCulloch*. In taking this role, the majority assumed that the vitality of the republic is constantly threatened by centrifugal forces, and the Court must be the ally of the other federal branches.").

[33] *Clinton*, 524 U.S. at 438.

[34] Aaron D. Zibart, *Eulogizing the Line Item Veto Act:* Clinton v. City of New York *and the Wisdom of Presidential Legislating* 88 KY. L.J. 505, 512 (1999). *See also* Eric Stephen Schmitt, Note, *There Is No Joy in D.C., the Mighty Court Struck Out: An Analysis of* Clinton v. City of New York, *the Line Item Veto Act and the Court's Failure to Uphold Constitutionally Legitimate Means to a Viable End*, 44 ST. LOUIS L.J. 167, 170 (2000) (noting that 43 out of 50 governors had the line item veto by the late 1980s).

[35] P.L. 104-130, 110 Stat. 1200 (Apr. 9, 1996) (codified at 2 U.S.C. § 691 et seq. (1994 ed., Supp. II)).

[36] Raines v. Byrd, 521 U.S. 811, 830 (1997). *See also* Nat'l Treasury Employees Union v. United States, 101 F.3d 1423, 1425-26 (D.C. Cir. 1996) (finding that the plaintiffs lacked standing because they had not suffered concrete injury).

[37] *Raines*, 521 U.S. at 837 (Stevens, J., dissenting).

[38] *Clinton*, 524 U.S. at 422-25.

[39] *Compare id.* at 425-35 (finding that plaintiffs have standing) *with id.* at 453 (Scalia, J., dissenting) (finding that certain plaintiffs lack standing).

[40] *See, e.g.*, Lac Du Flambeau Flambeau Band v. Norton, 422 F.3d 490 (7th Cir. 2005); Freedom from Religion Found., Inc. v. Obama, 2010 U.S. Dist. LEXIS 18108 (W.D. Wisc. Mar. 1, 2010); Katin v. Nat'l Real Estate Info. Servs., 2009 U.S. Dist. LEXIS 31398 (D. Mass. Mar. 31, 2009). *See also* Schmitt, *supra* note 34, at 185 ("It should be noted ... that although *Clinton* will be remembered as the 'line item veto case,' its impact on the law of standing will be equally significant."). Justice Stevens's opinion is also sometimes cited for its approach to statutory interpretation. *See, e.g.*, United States v. Middleton, 231 F.3d 1207 (9th Cir. 2000).

[41] *Clinton*, 524 U.S. at 438. *See also id.* at 439 ("[C]onstitutional silence on this profoundly important issue [is] equivalent to an express prohibition.").

[42] *Id.* at 438-39 ("The constitutional return takes place *before* the bill becomes law; the statutory cancellation occurs *after* the bill becomes law. The constitutional return is of the entire bill; the statutory cancellation is of only a part.").

[43] *Id.* at 439-40 (quoting the writings of the first President, George Washington, to show that the Bicameralism and Presentment Clauses were initially understood as requiring that the President either "approve all the parts of a Bill, or reject it in toto.").

[44] *Id.* at 440 (quoting *Chadha*, 462 U.S. 919, 951 (1983)).

[45] *Id.* The dissenting justices, in contrast, would have characterized the Line Item Veto Act as authorizing the President to decline to spend certain funds, rather than repeal certain provisions of law. *See, e.g., id.* at 474-75 (Breyer, J., dissenting) ("[T]he Act does not delegate to the President the power truly to *cancel* a line item expenditure (returning the legal status quo to one in which the item had never been enacted). Rather, it delegates to the President the power to decide *how* to spend the money to which the line item refers.").

[46] *Id.* at 442-47.

[47] *Id.* at 448 ("[B]ecause we conclude that the Act's cancellation provisions violate Article I, § 7, of the Constitution, we find it unnecessary to consider the District Court's alternative holding that the Act 'impermissibly disrupts the balance of powers among the three branches of government.'").

[48] *Id.* at 479-96 (Breyer, J., dissenting).

[49] *Id.* at 465-69. Justice Scalia focused particularly upon the fact that Presidents have historically claimed and exercised authority to withhold appropriated funds even without being expressly authorized by Congress to do so. He viewed this authority as differing in name only from the authority allegedly given to the President by the Line Item Veto Act.

[50] *Id.* at 482 (Breyer, J., dissenting) (quoting *Buckley v. Valeo*, 424 U.S. 1, 122 (1976)).

[51] *See, e.g.*, Bowsher v. Synar, 478 U.S. 714 (1986) (striking down a statute that authorized a legislative branch official to impose certain budget reductions on the President in the event that the budget exceeded allowable deficits); Northern Pipeline Constr. Co. v. Marathon Pipe Line Co., 458 U.S. 50, 73 (1982) (holding that Congress cannot give Article III "judicial" power to an Article I judge); Myers v. United States, 272 U.S. 52 (1926) (Congress cannot limit the President's power to remove an executive branch official).

[52] United States v. Chicago, M., St. P. & P. R. Co., 282 U.S. 311, 324 (1931). *See also* J.W. Hampton, Jr., & Co. v. United States, 276 U.S. 394, 409 (holding that the Constitution permits only those delegations where Congress "lay[s] down by legislative act an intelligible principle to which the person or body authorized to [act] is directed to conform."). Some commentators have suggested that the Court looks less favorably upon congressional delegation of legislative power than it formerly did. *See, e.g.*, Hugo Heclo,

What Has Happened to the Separation of Powers? in SEPARATION OF POWERS AND GOOD GOVERNMENT 131, 136 (Bradford P. Wilson & Peter W. Schramm eds., 1994).

[53] *Clinton*, 524 U.S. at 445-46.

[54] This view is shared by some commentators. *See, e.g.*, Friedelbaum, *supra* note 2, at 1576 (crediting Justice Stevens's opinion in *Term Limits* with introducing an "updated version of American federalism"); Sullivan, *supra* note 3, at 108 ("[T]he majority in *Term Limits* can be expected to continue to invalidate state laws that burden federal citizens, even in the absence of express or implied congressional preemption.").

[55] Sullivan, *supra* note 3, at 102 (characterizing this revival as one "of uncertain scope and consequence"). *See also* Linda Greenhouse, *Focus on Federal Power*, N.Y. TIMES, May 24, 1995, at A1 (describing the dissenting Justices in *Term Limits* as approaching "something radically different from the modern understanding of the Constitution"); Jeffrey Rosen, *Terminated*, NEW REPUBLIC, June 12, 1995, at 12 (suggesting that the dissenters are questioning "the legacy of Reconstruction"); Chris Marks, Comment, U.S. Term Limits, Inc. v. Thornton *and* United States v. Lopez: *The Supreme Court Resuscitates the Tenth Amendment*, 68 U. COLO. L. REV. 541, 541 (1997) ("In the 1994-95 Term, ... the U.S. Supreme Court resuscitated the long dormant Tenth Amendment."). Justice Stevens's opinion in *Term Limits* has also influenced lower courts in determining whether particular ballot access or other provisions constitute "impermissible indirect attempts" to impose additional qualifications on Members of Congress. Courts relying on *Term Limits* here have construed its holding that "a state amendment is unconstitutional when it has the likely effect of handicapping a class of candidates and has the sole purpose of creating additional qualifications indirectly" as establishing a two-part test for identifying such attempts. *See, e.g.*, Gralike v. Cook, 191 F.3d 911 (8th Cir. 1999) (striking down an amendment to the Missouri Constitution that would have required ballots to carry labels noting that particular legislators "disregarded voters' instruction on term limits"); Schaefer v. Townsend, 215 F.3d 1031 (9th Cir. 2000) (striking down a California law that required congressional candidates to live in the state for a certain time before the election); Cartwright v. Barnes, 304 F.3d 1138 (11th Cir. 2002) (upholding a Georgia law requiring that federal candidates obtain signatures from a certain percentage of registered voters to appear on the ballot).

[56] *Lopez*, 514 U.S. 549, 567 (1995). Justice Stevens dissented in *Lopez*.

[57] See *supra* note 29 and accompanying text. Justice Kennedy is the only Justice to have voted with the majority in both *Lopez* and *Term Limits*.

[58] *See, e.g.*, Marks, *supra* note 55, at 541; Sullivan, *supra* note 3, at 102. *See also* Sullivan, *supra* note 3, at 106 ("Narrow interpretation of Congress's commerce power is the flip side of imposing on Congress an external, federalism-based constraint: both protect the states from the reach of federal legislative power.").

[59] 529 U.S. 598 (2000) (finding that Congress lacked authority to enact the Violence against Women Act under either the Commerce Clause or the Fourteenth Amendment. This Commerce Clause jurisprudence has itself arguably been somewhat limited by *Raich v. Gonzales*, which held that the Commerce Clause allows Congress to ban home-grown cannabis even in states that have approved its use for medicinal purposes. *Raich*, 545 U.S. 1 (2005)).

[60] *Contra* Marks, *supra* note 55, at 570 ("More significant and immediate change will most likely be seen in cases falling outside the Commerce Clause. The Court may find ways, through a resuscitated Tenth Amendment, to empower states on such issues as immigration or affirmative action.").

[61] *See, e.g.*, Sullivan, *supra* note 3, at 93; Zibart, *supra* note 34, at 511 (characterizing Justice Breyer's opinion, in contrast, as "embrac[ing] more diffuse notions of the boundaries between the federal branches"); Henry L. Chambers, Jr. & Dennis E. Logue, Jr., *Separation of Powers and the 1995-1996 Budget Impasse*, 16 ST. LOUIS U. PUB. L. REV. 51, 55 (1996) ("Unfortunately, the Court may show similar disregard for carefully negotiated political agreements which probe the boundaries of the separation of powers.").

In: Jurisprudence of Supreme Court Justice... ISBN: 978-1-61761-282-4
Editor: Harvey B. Lymont

Chapter 3

THE JURISPRUDENCE OF JUSTICE JOHN PAUL STEVENS: SELECTED OPINIONS ON INTELLECTUAL PROPERTY LAW

Brian T. Yeh

SUMMARY

This chapter briefly surveys decisions of retiring Justice John Paul Stevens in intellectual property cases. An examination of Justice Stevens' written opinions relating to intellectual property law reveals a strong desire to ensure that the rights of intellectual property creators are balanced with the rights of the public to access creative and innovative works. No decision embodies this interest more than Justice Stevens' majority opinion in *Sony Corporation of America v. Universal City Studios, Inc.*, a landmark copyright case issued in 1984 that paved the way for the development and sale of popular consumer electronics, such as the video recorder (VCR, DVR, TiVo), portable music and video players (iPod), personal computers, and other devices that permit the recording and playback of copyrighted content.

In addition, Justice Stevens issued a lengthy dissent in the 2003 case *Eldred v. Ashcroft*, in which he asserted that Congress lacked the power to pass a law that extended the term of existing copyrights by 20 years. Such a retroactive extension delays the entrance of copyrighted works into the public domain and, in Justice Stevens' opinion, is a violation of the Constitution's

Copyright Clause that authorizes Congress to grant exclusive intellectual property rights to authors and artists for "limited Times."

In the area of patent law, Justice Stevens authored the majority opinion in the 1978 case *Parker v. Flook* that sought to severely restrict the availability of patent protection on inventions relating to computer software programs. Yet just three years later, the Supreme Court's decision in *Diamond v. Diehr* effectively opened the door to the allowance of patents on some computer programs. Justice Stevens wrote a strongly worded dissent in *Diehr* in which he suggested that Congress would be better suited than the Court to address the policy considerations of allowing patent protection for computer programs. His written opinions in both of these cases reveal an interest in judicial restraint, not wanting to extend patent rights into areas that Congress had not contemplated.

Justice Stevens dissented from the 1999 opinion, *Florida Prepaid v. College Savings Bank*, in which a majority of the Court invalidated Congress's attempt to abrogate state sovereign immunity and authorize patent holders to file suits for monetary damages against states and state instrumentalities that infringe their patent rights. Justice Stevens believed that the 1992 Patent and Plant Variety Protection Remedy Clarification Act was a proper exercise of Congress's authority under §5 of the Fourteenth Amendment to prevent state deprivations of property without due process of law, and he expressed his disagreement with the majority opinion's expansive protection of states' rights.

INTRODUCTION

Retiring Justice John Paul Stevens has not authored many opinions relating to intellectual property law, but those he has written reflect his interest in striking an appropriate balance between the protection of intellectual property rights and public access to the products of creative and inventive minds. His intellectual property opinions seek to serve the central purposes of the Copyright and Patent Clause of the Constitution—(1) encourage and reward the creativity of authors and inventors by offering them exclusive legal rights to their respective writings and discoveries, and (2) promote the progress of science and useful arts by requiring that the monopoly privileges last only for a limited period, after which the public gains free access to such work. This chapter examines Justice Stevens' opinions involving copyright law, patent law, and state sovereign immunity and patent infringement lawsuits. A brief summary of the basic principles and provisions of copyright and patent law precedes each section describing these opinions.

COPYRIGHT LAW OPINIONS

Copyright is a federal grant of legal protection for certain original works of creative expression, including books, movies, photography, art, and music.[1] The Copyright Act refers to the creator of such works as an "author;" ownership of a copyright initially vests in the author,[2] but the author may transfer ownership of the copyright to another person or company.[3] A copyright holder possesses several exclusive legal entitlements under the Copyright Act, which together provide the holder with the right to determine whether and under what circumstances the protected work may be used by third parties. The grant of copyright permits the copyright holder to exercise, or authorize others to exercise, the following exclusive rights:

- the reproduction of the copyrighted work;
- the preparation of derivative works based on the copyrighted work;
- the distribution of copies of the copyrighted work;
- the public performance of the copyrighted work; and
- the public display of the copyrighted work, including the individual images of a motion picture.[4]

Therefore, a party desiring to reproduce, adapt, distribute, publicly display, or publicly perform a copyrighted work must ordinarily obtain the permission of the copyright holder, which is usually granted in the form of a voluntarily negotiated license agreement that establishes conditions of use and an amount of monetary compensation known as a royalty fee. There are, however, other ways a third party may legally use a copyrighted work in the absence of affirmative permission from the copyright holder, including the use of statutory licenses or reliance upon the "fair use" doctrine.

The doctrine of "fair use" recognizes the right of the public to make reasonable use of copyrighted material, under particular circumstances, without the copyright holder's consent. For example, a teacher may be able to use reasonable excerpts of copyrighted works in preparing a scholarly lecture or commentary, without obtaining permission to do so. The Copyright Act mentions fair use "for purposes such as criticism, comment, news reporting, teaching, scholarship, or research."[5] However, a determination of fair use by a court considers four factors:

- the purpose and character of the use including whether such use is of a commercial nature or is for nonprofit educational purposes,
- the nature of the copyrighted work,
- the amount and substantiality of the portion used in relation to the copyrighted work as a whole, and
- the effect of the use upon the potential market for or value of the copyrighted work.[6]

Because the language of the fair use statute is illustrative, determining what constitutes a fair use of a copyrighted work is often difficult to make in advance—according to the U.S. Supreme Court, such a determination requires a federal court to engage in "case-by-case" analysis.[7]

Violation of one of the exclusive rights of the copyright holder constitutes infringement, and the copyright holder may bring a civil lawsuit against the alleged infringer to collect monetary damages and/or to obtain an injunction to prevent further infringement.[8] The direct infringer is not the only party potentially liable for infringement; the federal courts have recognized two forms of secondary copyright infringement liability: contributory and vicarious. The concept of contributory infringement has its roots in tort law and the notion that one should be held accountable for directly contributing to another's infringement.[9] For contributory infringement liability to exist, a court must find that the secondary infringer "with knowledge of the infringing activity, induces, causes or materially contributes to the infringing conduct of another."[10] Vicarious infringement liability is possible where a defendant "has the right and ability to supervise the infringing activity and also has a direct financial interest in such activities."[11]

Fair Use and Consumer Electronics

For manufacturers of consumer electronics and personal computers, the Supreme Court's 1984 decision in *Sony Corporation of America v. Universal City Studios*[12] is considered the "Magna Carta" of product innovation and the technology age.[13] The *Sony* decision held that the sale of the home video cassette recorder (VCR) did not constitute contributory infringement of the copyrights on television programs, because such a "staple article of commerce" is capable of "substantial noninfringing uses"[14] that include "time-shifting"—recording a television program to view it once at a later time, and thereafter erasing it.[15] *Sony's* embrace of time-shifting as a "fair use" of copyrighted works has created a safe harbor from copyright infringement liability for developers and sellers of electronic devices that facilitate the recording, storage, and playback of copyrighted media, such as the digital video recorder (DVR and TiVo), portable music and video players (iPod), and personal computers.[16] Some commentators consider the *Sony* decision to be the "legal foundation of the Digital Age."[17] The outcome of *Sony* "meant that companies could invest in the development of new digital technologies without incurring the risk of enormous liability for the potential misuses of those technologies by some of their consumers."[18]

The *Sony* case concerned a lawsuit in which owners of copyrights on broadcast television programs sought to hold Sony Corporation liable for contributory copyright infringement due to its manufacture and sale of the Betamax VCR that Betamax customers used to record some of the broadcasts.[19] The district court ruled in favor of Sony because the court concluded that noncommercial home recording of material broadcast over public airwaves was a fair use of copyrighted works.[20] The U.S. Court of Appeals for the Ninth Circuit disagreed, believing that the home use of a video tape recorder was not a fair use because it allowed for mass copying of copyrighted television programming.[21] The appellate court held that the copyright owners were entitled to appropriate relief, including an injunction against the manufacture and marketing of the Betamax video recorder or royalties on the sale of the equipment.[22]

The Supreme Court reversed the Ninth Circuit. Justice Stevens authored the majority opinion that garnered the support of four other justices. He was concerned that the Ninth Circuit's ruling, "if affirmed, would enlarge the scope of respondents' statutory monopolies to encompass control over an article of commerce that is not the subject of copyright protection. Such an expansion of the copyright privilege is beyond the limits of the grants authorized by Congress."[23] He explained that defining the scope of the copyright monopoly grant "involves a difficult balance between the interests of authors ... in the control and exploitation of their writings ... on the one hand, and society's competing interest in the free flow of ideas, information, and commerce on the other hand." Justice Stevens also noted that historically, Congress has been primarily responsible for amending copyright law in response to changes in technology.[24] He elaborated:

> The judiciary's reluctance to expand the protections afforded by the copyright without explicit legislative guidance is a recurring theme. Sound policy, as well as history, supports our consistent deference to Congress when major technological innovations alter the market for copyrighted materials. Congress has the constitutional authority and the institutional ability to accommodate fully the varied permutations of competing interests that are inevitably implicated by such new technology.[25]

While Justice Stevens observed that the "Copyright Act does not expressly render anyone liable for infringement committed by another,"[26] he nevertheless acknowledged that the lack of such statutory authorization does not preclude the imposition of vicarious liability on parties who have not themselves engaged in infringing activity.[27] He observed that the only contact between Sony and its customers occurs at the moment of sale of the Betamax video recorder. The video equipment may be used for both infringing and noninfringing purposes, as it is "generally capable of copying the entire range of programs that may be televised: those that are uncopyrighted, those that are copyrighted but may be copied without objection from the copyright holder, and those that the copyright holder would prefer not to have copied."[28]

As there was no precedent in copyright law for imposing vicarious liability on Sony because it sold the video recording equipment with constructive knowledge that its customers might use it to make unauthorized copies of copyrighted programming, Justice Stevens sought guidance from patent law, defending the appropriateness of such reference "because of the historic kinship between patent law and copyright law."[29] He first found that the Patent Act contained an express provision that prohibits contributory infringement liability in the case of the sale of a "staple article or commodity of commerce suitable for substantial noninfringing use."[30] He then quoted from an earlier Supreme Court case involving contributory patent infringement that had said "a sale of an article which though adapted to an infringing use is also adapted to other and lawful uses, is not enough to make the seller a contributory infringer. Such a rule would block the wheels of commerce."[31] While recognizing that there are differences between copyright and patent laws, Justice Stevens believed that the contributory infringement doctrine as it is used in patent law should also be applied to copyright law.[32] Therefore, he "imported" the "staple article of commerce doctrine" from patent law into copyright law,[33] in the passage below:

> The staple article of commerce doctrine must strike a balance between a copyright holder's legitimate demand for effective – not merely symbolic –

> protection of the statutory monopoly, and the rights of others freely to engage in substantially unrelated areas of commerce. Accordingly, the sale of copying equipment, like the sale of other articles of commerce, does not constitute contributory infringement if the product is widely used for legitimate, unobjectionable purposes. Indeed, it need merely be capable of substantial noninfringing uses.[34]

With this test articulated, Justice Stevens analyzed whether the Betamax was capable of commercially significant noninfringing uses. He identified one potential use that met this standard: "private, noncommercial time-shifting in the home."[35] Such time-shifting could be "authorized" time-shifting (recording noncopyrighted programs or material whose owners did not object to the copying) as well as unauthorized time-shifting (where the copyright holders did not consent to the practice). However, in his view, even unauthorized time-shifting is not infringing because such activity falls within the scope of the Copyright Act's "fair use" doctrine.[36] Because the Betamax is capable of substantial noninfringing uses, Sony's manufacture and sale of such equipment to the public did not constitute contributory copyright infringement.[37] Justice Stevens concluded the Court's majority opinion as follows:

> One may search the Copyright Act in vain for any sign that the elected representatives of the millions of people who watch television every day have made it unlawful to copy a program for later viewing at home, or have enacted a flat prohibition against the sale of machines that make such copying possible.
>
> It may well be that Congress will take a fresh look at this new technology, just as it so often has examined other innovations in the past. But it is not our job to apply laws that have not yet been written. Applying the copyright statute, as it now reads, to the facts as they have been developed in this case, the judgment of the Court of Appeals must be reversed.[38]

Extension of Copyright Terms

The Copyright Clause of the Constitution[39] authorizes Congress: "To promote the Progress of Science[40] ... by securing for limited Times to Authors ... the exclusive Right to their respective Writings...." Therefore, this constitutional provision indicates that the rights conferred by a copyright cannot last forever; rather, a copyright holder may exercise his/her exclusive rights only for "limited Times." At the expiration of that period of time, the copyrighted work becomes part of the public domain, available for anyone to use without payment of royalties or permission.

In 1790, the First Congress created a copyright term of 14 years for existing and future works, subject to renewal for a total of 28 years. By 1909, both the original and the renewal term had been extended to 28 years, for a combined term of 56 years. Additional extensions were enacted between 1962 and 1974. When the current Copyright Act was enacted in 1976, Congress revised the format of copyright terms to conform with the Berne Convention and international practice. Instead of a fixed-year term, the duration of copyright was established as the life of the author plus 50 years.

In 1998, Congress passed the Copyright Term Extension Act (CTEA)[41] that added 20 years to the term of copyright for both subsisting and future copyrights to bring U.S. copyright terms more closely into conformance with those governed by the European Union. Hence, the law currently provides that an author of a creative work may enjoy copyright protection for the work for a term lasting the entirety of his/her life plus 70 additional years.[42]

Plaintiffs representing individuals and businesses that rely upon and utilize materials in the public domain filed a lawsuit against the U.S. Attorney General to obtain a declaration that the CTEA is unconstitutional. Among other things, plaintiffs argued that in extending the term of subsisting copyrights, the CTEA violated the "limited Times" requirement of the Copyright Clause. The lower court held in favor of the Attorney General, finding no constitutional problems.[43] The U.S. Court of Appeals for the District of Columbia Circuit affirmed the district court.[44]

Justice Ginsburg wrote the majority opinion in *Eldred v. Ashcroft*,[45] in which the Court upheld the CTEA by a vote of 7-2.[46] She stated that "[h]istory reveals an unbroken congressional practice of granting to authors the benefit of term extensions so that all under copyright protection will be governed evenhandedly under the same regime."[47] She rejected the plaintiffs' argument that the "limited Times" requirement requires a forever "fixed" or "inalterable" copyright term.[48] Ultimately, the Court found that the unbroken congressional practice for more than two centuries of applying adjustments to copyright term to both existing and future works "is almost conclusive."[49]

Justice Stevens wrote a vigorous dissent in *Eldred*; Justice Breyer filed a separate dissenting opinion. Justice Stevens concluded that *any* extension of the life of an existing copyright beyond its expiration date exceeds Congress's authority under the Copyright Clause.[50] He noted that the Copyright Clause was "both a grant of power and a limitation," and that the "limited Times" requirement serves the purpose of promoting the progress of science by ensuring that authors' creative works will enter the public domain once the period of exclusivity expires.[51] He criticized the majority opinion's reliance on the history of Congress's "unbroken pattern" of applying copyright extensions retroactively, arguing that "the fact that Congress has repeatedly acted on a mistaken interpretation of the Constitution does not qualify our duty to invalidate an unconstitutional practice when it is finally challenged in an appropriate case."[52] Justice Stevens opined that "[e]x post facto extensions of copyrights result in a gratuitous transfer of wealth from the public to authors, publishers, and their successors in interest. Such retroactive extensions do not even arguably serve ... the purpose[] of the Copyright ... Clause."[53] He concluded his dissent by making this observation:

> By failing to protect the public interest in free access to the products of inventive and artistic genius – indeed, by virtually ignoring the central purpose of the Copyright... Clause – the Court has quitclaimed to Congress its principal responsibility in this area of the law. Fairly read, the Court has stated that Congress' actions under the Copyright ... Clause are, for all intents and purposes, judicially unreviewable. That result cannot be squared with the basic tenets of our constitutional structure.[54]

Patent Law Opinions

According to section 101 of the Patent Act, one who "invents or discovers any new and useful process, machine, manufacture, or any composition of matter, or any new and useful improvement thereof, may obtain a patent therefore, subject to the conditions and requirements of this title."[55] Thus, the subject matter that is eligible for patent protection may be divided into four categories: processes, machines, manufactures, and compositions of matter. The statutory scope of patentable subject matter under § 101 of the Patent Act is quite expansive—the U.S. Supreme Court once observed that the legislative history describing the intent of § 101 was to make patent protection available to "anything under the sun that is made by man."[56]

Notwithstanding the breadth of patentable subject matter, the Supreme Court has articulated certain limits to § 101, stating that "laws of nature, natural phenomena, and abstract ideas" may not be patented.[57] The Court has elaborated on this restriction in several cases, including the following explanation:

> [A] new mineral discovered in the earth or a new plant found in the wild is not patentable subject matter. Likewise, Einstein could not patent his celebrated law that $E=mc^2$; nor could Newton have patented the law of gravity. Such discoveries are "manifestations of ... nature, free to all men and reserved exclusively to none."[58]

Process patents (also called method patents) involve an act, or series of steps, that may be performed to achieve a given result.[59] The Patent Act defines a "process" to mean a "process, art, or method, and includes a new use of a known process, machine, manufacture, composition of matter, or material."[60] However, this statutory definition is not particularly illuminating "given that the definition itself uses the term 'process.'"[61] It has thus been up to the courts to interpret the scope of patentable processes under § 101 of the Patent Act.

Computer Software Patents

Software-related inventions may be patented if they meet the statutory requirements of the Patent Act.[62] Today more than 20,000 software patents are granted each year. While software patents comprised approximately 2% of all patents awarded in the early 1980s, they now account for approximately 15% of the total number of U.S. patent issued each year.[63]

At the dawn of the computer age in the 1970s, however, inventions relating to computer software were ineligible for patent protection due to a 1972 Supreme Court case, *Gottschalk v. Benson*. The *Benson* Court held that mathematical algorithms, though they may be novel and useful, may not be patented.[64] The Court rejected patent claims for an algorithm used to convert binary code decimal numbers to equivalent pure binary numbers (in order to program a computer), because such claims "were not limited to any particular art or technology, to any particular apparatus or machinery, or to any particular end use."[65] A patent on such claims, according to the Court, "would wholly pre-empt the mathematical formula and in practical effect would be a patent on the algorithm itself."[66] The *Benson* Court then pronounced that "[p]henomena of nature, though just discovered, mental processes, and abstract intellectual concepts are not patentable, as they are the basic tools of scientific and technological work."[67]

After *Benson*, patent applicants tried to obtain patents on mechanical devices and processes that included the use of a computer program to run the machine or implement the process.[68] In a 1978 case, *Parker v. Flook*,[69] Justice Stevens wrote the majority opinion, joined by five other justices, in which the Court rejected this attempt to runaround *Benson*. In *Flook*, the patent application described a method for computing an "alarm limit," which is a number that may signal the presence of an abnormal condition in temperature, pressure, and flow rates during catalytic conversion processes.[70] Justice Stevens criticized the patent claims, as follows:

> The patent application does not purport to explain how to select the appropriate margin of safety, the weighting factor, or any of the other variables. Nor does it purport to contain any disclosure relating to the chemical processes at work, the monitoring of process variables, or the means of setting off an alarm or adjusting an alarm system. All that it provides is a formula for computing an updated alarm limit. Although the computations can be made by pencil and paper calculations, ... the formula is primarily useful for computerized calculations producing automatic adjustments in alarm settings.[71]

Although the patent applicant attempted to distinguish the case from *Benson* by pointing out that his application called for "post-solution" activity—the adjustment of the alarm limit to the figure computed according to the formula—Justice Stevens rejected this argument:

> The notion that post-solution activity, no matter how conventional or obvious in itself, can transform an unpatentable principle into a patentable process exalts form over substance. A competent draftsman could attach some form of post-solution activity to almost any mathematical formula; the Pythagorean theorem would not have been patentable, or partially patentable, because a patent application contained a final step indicating that the formula, when solved, could be usefully applied to existing surveying techniques.[72]

While he allowed that an "inventive application" of a mathematical formula may be patented, he determined that the Flook's application contained no claim of patentable invention.[73] Rather, the application "simply provides a new and presumably better method for calculating alarm limit values."[74] He then concluded that "a claim for an improved method of calculation, even when tied to a specific end use, is unpatentable subject matter under § 101."[75] However, Justice Stevens commented at the end of his opinion:

> To a large extent our conclusion is based on reasoning derived from opinions written before the modern business of developing programs for computers was conceived. The youth of the industry may explain the complete absence of precedent supporting patentability. Neither the dearth of precedent, nor this decision, should therefore be interpreted as reflecting a judgment that patent protection of certain novel and useful computer programs will not promote the progress of science and the useful arts, or that such protection is undesirable as a matter of policy. Difficult questions of policy concerning the kinds of programs that may be appropriate for patent protection and the form and duration of such protection can be answered by Congress on the basis of current empirical data not equally available to this tribunal.
>
> It is our duty to construe the patent statutes as they now read, in light of our prior precedents, and we must proceed cautiously when we are asked to extend patent rights into areas wholly unforeseen by Congress.[76]

Only three years after *Flook*, the Supreme Court issued a 5-4 decision that appears to conflict with *Flook*. The opinion of the Court in *Diamond v. Diehr*[77] was written by Justice Rehnquist, who had dissented in *Flook*.[78] The *Diehr* Court upheld the patentability of a computer program-controlled process for producing cured synthetic rubber products, stating:

> [A] physical and chemical process for molding precision synthetic rubber products falls within the § 101 categories of possibly patentable subject matter. That respondents' claims involve the transformation of an article, in this case raw, uncured synthetic rubber, into a different state or thing cannot be disputed. The respondents' claims describe in detail a step-by-step method for accomplishing such, beginning with the loading of a mold with raw, uncured rubber and ending with the eventual opening of the press at the conclusion of the cure. Industrial processes such as this are the types which have historically been eligible to receive the protection of our patent laws.[79]

The fact that several of the process's steps involved the use of a mathematical formula and a programmed digital computer did *not* pose a barrier to patent eligibility, according to the *Diehr* Court:

> [T]he respondents here do not seek to patent a mathematical formula. Instead, they seek patent protection for a process of curing synthetic rubber. Their process admittedly employs a well-known mathematical equation, but they do not seek to pre-empt the use of that equation. Rather, they seek only

> to foreclose from others the use of that equation in conjunction with all of the other steps in their claimed process.[80]

Finally, the Court concluded that "a claim drawn to subject matter otherwise statutory does not become nonstatutory simply because it uses a mathematical formula, computer program, or digital computer."[81]

Justice Stevens wrote a lengthy dissent in *Diehr*, joined by three other justices who were in the *Flook* majority. He noted that the *Benson* decision in 1972 had "clearly held that new mathematical procedures that can be conducted in old computers, like mental processes and abstract intellectual concepts ... are not patentable processes within the meaning of § 101."[82] In Justice Stevens' view, Diehr's patent claim concerning a method of using a computer to determine the amount of time a rubber molding press should remain closed during the synthetic rubber-curing process "is strikingly reminiscent" of the method of updating alarm limits that the Court had held unpatentable in *Flook*.[83] He argued that "[t]he broad question whether computer programs should be given patent protection involves policy considerations that this Court is not authorized to address."[84] Justice Stevens would have preferred that the Court's opinion contained the following:

> (1) an unequivocal holding that no program-related invention is a patentable process under §101 unless it makes a contribution to the art that is not dependent entirely on the utilization of a computer, and (2) an unequivocal explanation that the term "algorithm" as used in this case, as in *Benson* and *Flook*, is synonymous with the term "computer program."[85]

The *Diehr* decision and its appellate progeny encouraged software patent applicants to follow "the doctrine of the magic words," whereby the applicant could obtain a patent on software inventions "only if the applicant recited the magic words and pretended that she was patenting something else entirely," such as hardware devices, some sort of apparatus, or other machines.[86] However, in 1994 the U.S. Court of Appeals for the Federal Circuit, which has exclusive appellate jurisdiction in patent cases,[87] did away with this charade. The Federal Circuit issued an en banc decision, *In re Alappat*, in which it concluded that "a computer operating pursuant to software may represent patentable subject matter."[88]

STATE SOVEREIGN IMMUNITY AND PATENT INFRINGEMENT

The Patent Act grants patent holders the right to exclude others from making, using, offering for sale, or selling their patented invention throughout the United States, or importing the invention into the United States.[89] Whoever performs any one of these five acts during the term of the invention's patent, without the patent holder's authorization, is liable for infringement.[90] Defendants who may be sued for patent infringement include private individuals, companies, and also the federal government.[91]

Yet when state governments and state institutions (such as state-owned universities) infringe patents, the patent holder currently has very limited legal recourse because of the U.S. Supreme Court's jurisprudence concerning the Eleventh Amendment to the U.S. Constitution.[92] The Eleventh Amendment, with limited exceptions, bars an individual from suing a state under federal law without the state's consent. While states may consent to suit by waiving the privilege of sovereign immunity, in limited circumstances Congress may also abrogate, or overrule, that immunity by passing a statute pursuant to the enforcement power under § 5 of the Fourteenth Amendment.[93]

Patent Remedy Act

Congress passed the Patent and Plant Variety Protection Remedy Clarification Act (Patent Remedy Act) in 1992.[94] The language of the statute specifically and unequivocally abrogated state sovereign immunity and subjected the states to suits for monetary damages brought by individuals for violation of federal patent law. The validity of this statute was challenged in *Florida Prepaid v. College Savings Bank*.[95]

College Savings Bank held a patent for its financing methodology, based on certificates of deposit and annuity contracts, designed to guarantee investors funds for future college expenses. The state of Florida soon adopted College Savings Bank's methodology and created the Florida Prepaid Postsecondary Education Expense Board (the Board) to issue similar financing options to its own residents. Consequently, College Savings Bank filed a claim for patent infringement against the Board under the Patent Remedy Act. The principal issue in *Florida Prepaid* was whether the Patent Remedy Act had legitimately abrogated state sovereign immunity from suit for patent infringement. College Savings Bank argued that Congress had lawfully done so pursuant to the due process clause by ensuring an individual an adequate remedy in the case of a deprivation of property perpetrated by the state in the form of patent infringement.

The district court agreed with College Savings Bank, and the Federal Circuit Court affirmed. However, the Supreme Court, in a 5-4 decision, overturned the Federal Circuit decision, holding that the PRCA was *not* a valid use of the § 5 enforcement power of the Fourteenth Amendment and therefore *not* a legitimate abrogation of state sovereign immunity.[96]

Justice Stevens filed a dissenting opinion, joined by three other justices. He first observed that the Constitution vested Congress with plenary authority over patents, and that Congress had passed laws providing federal courts with exclusive jurisdiction of patent infringement litigation.[97] He noted that there is "a strong federal interest in an interpretation of the patent statutes that is ... uniform," and that such federal interest is "threatened ... by inadequate protection for patentees."[98] In Justice Stevens' view, it was "appropriate for Congress to abrogate state sovereign immunity in patent infringement cases in order to close a potential loophole in the uniform federal scheme, which, if undermined, would necessarily decrease the efficacy of the process afforded to patent holders."[99] He believed that the Patent Remedy Act was a proper exercise of Congress's power under §5 of the Fourteenth Amendment to prevent state deprivations of property without due process of law.[100] Supporting the concern for potential due process violations, he referred to the legislative history of the Patent Remedy Act that included congressional findings that state remedies would be insufficient to compensate inventors whose patents had been infringed, and also that state infringement of patents was likely to increase.[101] Justice Stevens argued that the Patent Remedy Act "merely puts" states in the same position as the federal government and private users of the patent system when it comes to the possibility of being held accountable for patent infringement.[102]

At the conclusion of his dissent, Justice Stevens criticized the majority opinion's "aggressive sovereign immunity jurisprudence" that "demonstrates itself to be the champion of States' rights."[103]

End Notes

[1] 17 U.S.C. § 102(a).
[2] 17 U.S.C. § 201(a).

[3] 17 U.S.C. § 201(d).
[4] 17 U.S.C. § 106.
[5] 17 U.S.C. § 107.
[6] *Id.*
[7] Campbell v. Acuff-Rose Music, Inc., 510 U.S. 569, 577 (1994).
[8] 17 U.S.C. § 501.
[9] Fonovisa, Inc. v. Cherry Auction, Inc., 76 F.3d 259, 264 (9th Cir. 1996).
[10] A & M Records, Inc. v. Napster, Inc., 239 F.3d 1004, 1019 (9th Cir. 2001).
[11] Gershwin Publ'g Corp. v. Columbia Artists Mgmt, Inc., 443 F2d. 1159, 1162 (2d. Cir. 1971).
[12] 464 U.S. 417 (1984).
[13] Randal C. Picker, *Rewinding Sony: The Evolving Product, Phoning Home, and the Duty of Ongoing Design*, 55 CASE W. RES. L. REV. 749, 753 (2005); Jessica Litman, *The Sony Paradox*, 55 CASE W. RES. L. REV. 917, 951-60 (2005).
[14] *Sony*, 464 U.S. at 442, 456.
[15] *Id.* at 423.
[16] Peter Menell & David Nimmer, *Unwinding Sony*, 95 CAL. L. REV. 941, 943 (2007).
[17] Matt Schruers and Jonathan Band, *Justice Stevens Invented the Internet*, CCIA Innovation Policy Post, April 20, 2010, *at* http://www.ccianet.org/index. asp?bid=89&BlogEntryID=67&FormID=300&catid=0.
[18] *Id.*
[19] *Sony*, 464 U.S. at 419.
[20] *Id.* at 425.
[21] *Id.* at 427-28.
[22] *Id.* at 421.
[23] *Id.*
[24] *Id.* at 430-31.
[25] *Id.* at 431 (citations omitted).
[26] *Id.* at 434.
[27] *Id.* at 435.
[28] *Id.* at 436-37.
[29] *Id.* at 439.
[30] *Id.* at 440 (citing 35 U.S.C. § 271(c)).
[31] Henry v. A. B. Dick Co., 224 U.S. 1, 48 (1912).
[32] *Sony*, 464 U.S. at 442.
[33] Menell & Nimmer, *supra* note 17, at 993.
[34] *Sony*, 464 U.S. at 442.
[35] *Id.*
[36] *Id.* at 454-55.
[37] *Id.* at 456.
[38] *Id.*
[39] U.S. CONST., art. I, § 8, cl. 8.
[40] The Framers of the Constitution used the word "Science" to mean "learning or knowledge." Eldred v. Ashcroft, 537 U.S. 186, 243 (2003) (Breyer, J., dissenting).
[41] P.L. 105-298.
[42] 17 U.S.C. § 302. Other terms have been established for different works and different periods of time. For a concise chart explaining the different terms, *see* http://www.copyright. cornell.edu/resources/publicdomain.cfm.
[43] Eldred v. Reno, 74 F. Supp.2d 1 (D.D.C. 1999).
[44] Eldred v. Reno, 239 F.3d 372, 373 (D.C.Cir. 2001).
[45] 537 U.S. 186 (2003).
[46] For a more thorough analysis of this case, *see* CRS Report RS21179, *Copyright Term Extension: Eldred v. Ashcroft*, by Robin Jeweler.
[47] *Eldred*, 537 U.S. at 200.

[48] *Id.* at 199.
[49] *Id.* (citation omitted).
[50] *Id.* at 222-23 (Stevens, J., dissenting).
[51] *Id.* at 223.
[52] *Id.* at 235.
[53] *Id.* at 227.
[54] *Id.* at 242.
[55] 35 U.S.C. § 101.
[56] Diamond v. Chakrabarty, 447 U.S. 303, 309 (1980).
[57] Diamond v. Diehr, 450 U.S. 175, 185 (1981).
[58] *Chakrabarty*, 447 U.S. at 309 (quoting Funk Brothers Seed Co. v. Kalo Inoculant Co., 333 U.S. 127, 130 (1948)).
[59] *See* Cochrane v. Deener, 94 U.S. 780, 788 (1877) ("A process is a mode of treatment of certain materials to produce a given result. It is an act, or a series of acts, performed upon the subject-matter to be transformed and reduced to a different state or thing.").
[60] 35 U.S.C. § 100(b).
[61] In re Bilski, 545 F.3d 943, 951 n.3 (Fed. Cir. 2008).
[62] Julie E. Cohen & Mark A. Lemley, *Patent Scope and Innovation in the Software Industry*, 89 CAL. L. REV. 1, 8 (2001).
[63] James Bessen and Robert M. Hunt, *An Empirical Look at Software Patents, Working Paper No. 03-17/R, available at* http://www.researchoninnovation.org/swpat.pdf; Robert Hunt and James Bessen, *The Software Patent Experiment, available at* http://www.researchoninnovation.org/softpat.pdf. For more information on software patents, *see* CRS Report RL33367, *Patent Reform: Issues in the Biomedical and Software Industries*, by Wendy H. Schacht.
[64] 409 U.S. 63 (1972). For an extensive discussion of this case as well as software patents generally, *see* Pamela Samuelson, Benson *Revisited: The Case Against Patent Protection for Algorithms and Other Computer Program-Related Inventions*, 39 EMORY L.J. 1025 (1990).
[65] *Id.* at 64.
[66] *Id.* at 72.
[67] *Id.* at 67.
[68] Cohen & Lemley, *supra* note 52, at 9.
[69] 437 U.S. 584 (1978).
[70] *Id.* at 585.
[71] *Id.* at 586.
[72] *Id.* at 590.
[73] *Id.* at 594.
[74] *Id.*
[75] *Id.* at 595 n.18.
[76] *Id.* at 595.
[77] 450 U.S. 175 (1981).
[78] Justices Powell and White, after siding with Justice Stevens' in *Flook*, joined Justice Rehnquist's majority opinion in *Diehr*.
[79] *Id.* at 184.
[80] *Id.* at 187.
[81] *Id.*
[82] *Id.* at 201 (Stevens, J., dissenting) (citation omitted).
[83] *Id.* at 209.
[84] *Id.* at 217.
[85] *Id.* at 219.
[86] Cohen & Lemley, *supra* note 52, at 9.
[87] 28 U.S.C. § 1295(a)(1).

[88] 33 F.3d 1526, 1545 (Fed. Cir. 1994) (en banc).
[89] 35 U.S.C. §§ 154(a)(1), 271(a).
[90] 35 U.S.C. §§ 271, 281.
[91] The "federal government" referred to in this section includes not only agencies and instrumentalities of the federal government, but also a corporation owned or controlled by the United States, or a contractor, subcontractor, or any person, firm, or corporation acting for and with the authorization or consent of the federal government. *See* 28 U.S.C. § 1498(b); 15 U.S.C. § 1114(1).
[92] For detailed information regarding this topic, *see* CRS Report RL34593, *Infringement of Intellectual Property Rights and State Sovereign Immunity*, by Brian T. Yeh.
[93] Seminole Tribe of Florida v. Florida, 517 U.S. 44 (1996).
[94] P.L. 102-560, 106 Stat. 4230 (1992) (codified at 35 U.S.C. §§ 271(h), 296(a)).
[95] 527 U.S. 627 (1999).
[96] *Id.* at 647.
[97] *Id.* at 648 (Stevens, J., dissenting).
[98] *Id.* at 650.
[99] *Id.* at 652.
[100] *Id.* at 649.
[101] *Id.* at 656.
[102] *Id.* at 663.
[103] *Id.* at 664.

In: Jurisprudence of Supreme Court Justice... ISBN: 978-1-61761-282-4
Editor: Harvey B. Lymont

Chapter 4

THE JURISPRUDENCE OF JUSTICE JOHN PAUL STEVENS: LEADING OPINIONS ON WARTIME DETENTIONS

Anna C. Henning

SUMMARY

Justice John Paul Stevens played a pivotal role in determining the scope of executive-branch power in a post-9/11 world. After 9/11, Congress quickly authorized the Executive to respond to the terrorist attacks using military force. Difficult legal questions emerged from the consequences of the ensuing military actions, particularly as suspected members of Al Qaeda and the Taliban were captured in Afghanistan and elsewhere and transferred to the U.S. Naval Station at Guantanamo Bay, Cuba. Key questions included: What legal authorities restrict the Executive's ability to detain and try such persons as it sees fit? To what extent do detainees outside of the United States have the right to challenge their detentions in federal courts? When may Congress remove federal courts' jurisdiction over habeas cases?

Justice Stevens authored majority opinions in two leading cases, *Rasul v. Bush* and *Hamdan v. Rumsfeld*, in which the Court allowed detainees' habeas petitions to proceed and invalidated the early incarnation of military commissions, thereby rejecting the broader views of executive power articulated shortly after the 9/11 attacks. In the cases, his view prevailed over strongly articulated dissenting opinions authored by Justice Scalia and other justices.

For a more in-depth examination of the Supreme Court's post-9/11 decisions regarding habeas corpus, see CRS Report RL33180, *Enemy Combatant Detainees: Habeas Corpus Challenges in Federal Court*, by Jennifer K. Elsea and Michael John Garcia.

INTRODUCTION

Following the 9/11 terrorist attacks, Congress authorized the President's use of "all necessary and appropriate force" against those "nations, organizations, or persons" who "planned, authorized, committed, or aided the terrorist attacks."[1] As a result of subsequent military action, particularly in Afghanistan, the United States captured numerous persons whom it suspected of ties to Al Qaeda or the Taliban—groups alleged to have perpetrated the 9/11 attacks or to have aided the perpetrators. The United States transferred many such persons to the U.S. Naval Station at Guantanamo Bay, Cuba.

The Guantanamo detentions prompted difficult legal questions regarding wartime detention and the separation of powers, some of which had previously been explored only in the context of traditional wars. What legal frameworks limit the Executive's authority to detain and try persons captured in a military conflict as it sees fit? Do statutory and constitutional rights to challenge one's detention extend to non-citizens detained outside of the United States? In what circumstances may Congress limit the federal courts' jurisdiction over petitions for habeas corpus?

Justice Stevens has been a key player in the Supreme Court's resolution of such questions.[2] He authored majority opinions in two significant cases, *Rasul v. Bush*[3] and *Hamdan v. Rumsfeld*.[4] In those cases, the Court decided questions regarding Guantanamo detainees' access to habeas review on statutory grounds, without addressing whether the U.S. Constitution might guarantee such a right. Nevertheless, they arguably provided the legal underpinning for the 2008 decision *Boumediene v. Bush*,[5] in which the Court reached the constitutional question. Likewise, although the *Hamdan* decision struck down early military commission procedures on statutory grounds, it arguably framed the Court's approach to reviewing the balance of the three branches' powers during wartime and set the stage for future reviews of military commission procedures.

Justice Stevens might also be characterized as the leading voice among the justices encouraging the Court to rule on difficult separation-of-powers questions implicated by wartime detentions. In 2004, for example, he wrote a dissenting opinion, joined by three other justices, in *Rumsfeld v. Padilla*.[6] The case involved a man, determined by the President to be an enemy combatant, arrested in Chicago and detained in a military brig. The Court resolved his subsequent habeas challenge on statutory grounds, and did not resolve questions regarding the President's authority to conduct military detentions. In dissent, Justice Stevens argued that the Court had a duty to address the "questions of profound importance to the Nation" raised in the case.[7] He used relatively strong language to describe the importance of the questions at stake, concluding with the argument that "if this Nation is to remain true to the ideals symbolized by its flag, it must not wield the tools of tyrants even to resist an assault by the forces of tyranny."[8]

Historical Interpretation in Habeas Corpus Questions

Over time, the writ of habeas corpus has evolved as the primary means to challenge executive detentions. The U.S. Constitution does not mention the writ, except to limit the circumstances in which it may be suspended.[9] A federal statute, 28 U.S.C. § 2241, provides the federal courts with jurisdiction to grant writs of habeas corpus to specified petitioners, including those whose custody is shown to violate the U.S. Constitution, federal statute, or international law.[10] However, the writ has a history "antecedent to statute ... throwing its root deep into the genius of our common law."[11] Thus, the historical use and interpretation of the writ are crucial factors for interpreting its scope.

It is common for Supreme Court justices to emphasize history in their interpretation of the habeas writ; however, their views of history differ. A case decided shortly before the 9/11 attacks, *INS v. St. Cyr*,[12] offers a pre-9/11 glimpse of Justice Stevens's historical interpretation of the writ. In that case, a lawful permanent resident of the United States was subject to deportation by the executive branch because of an earlier conviction, but a legal issue arose on whether he was eligible for discretionary relief from removal. He filed a habeas petition in federal court to challenge his continued detention pending deportation. Although the case was resolved on statutory grounds, Justice

Stevens emphasized the traditional role the habeas writ plays in limiting executive-branch detention authority. Writing for the majority in the 5-4 case, he asserted that "[a]t its historical core, the writ of habeas corpus has served as a means of reviewing the legality of Executive detention...."[13] Contrasting petitions brought to challenge detentions initiated by the executive with petitions asserted in other contexts, including petitions filed by prisoners convicted by criminal courts,[14] he asserted that "it is in [the executive detention] context that [the writ's] protections have been the strongest."[15]

This view of the habeas writ's historical role appeared to inform Justice Stevens's approach in post-9/11 cases. For example, in *Hamdan*, he emphasized the "compelling historical precedent" supporting civilian courts' intervention in military commission proceedings.[16]

Contrast with Justice Scalia

Some commentators have characterized the post-9/11 wartime detention cases as evidencing a jurisprudential clash between Justice Stevens and Justice Scalia.[17] Nevertheless, though subsequently drawing differing conclusions from its application, the two justices have proceeded from a common analytical premise, as evidenced in *Hamdi v. Rumsfeld*,[18] one of the early landmark cases decided after the 9/11 attacks. In that case, a plurality of the Supreme Court justices upheld, with limitations,[19] the domestic detention of a U.S. citizen who was captured in Afghanistan and alleged to have been fighting for the Taliban. In a dissenting opinion, Justices Stevens and Scalia agreed on a position that none of the other justices shared. Specifically, they viewed the domestic, preventative (i.e., non-criminal) detention of a U.S. citizen as exceeding the Executive's power. The dissenting opinion articulated the most restrictive view of executive power among the various opinions. It asserted that, historically, "the Executive's assertion of military exigency has not been thought sufficient to permit detention without charge."[20]

However, as the factual scenarios moved beyond U.S. boundaries and involved non-citizens—including in *Rasul* (decided the very same day as *Hamdi*)—the two justices' interpretations diverged. Although both justices emphasized historical context and prior precedents, they reached opposite conclusions. Specifically, whereas Justice Stevens continued to interpret executive authority relatively narrowly as applied to non-citizens in Guantanamo, Justice Scalia perceived a historical distinction between the treatment of detainees on U.S. soil, on one hand, and the treatment of aliens outside U.S. territory, on the other hand. That difference is evident throughout the post-9/11 wartime detention cases. In several dissenting opinions, Justice Scalia argued in favor of bright-line rules, in which jurisdiction would end at the boundaries of U.S. sovereign territory. In contrast, Justice Stevens adopted a more case-specific approach, in which history and precedents were viewed as supporting the application of rights and jurisdiction to Guantanamo detainees.

One result of this split was that if Justice Scalia's approach had prevailed in the post-9/11 cases, the Court would have resolved many of the wartime detention cases by declining to exercise jurisdiction. Instead, Justice Stevens's approach led to the Court's resolution of various questions on the merits.

Rasul v. Bush

After 9/11, numerous Guantanamo detainees submitted habeas petitions in federal courts to challenge their detentions. The petition in *Rasul* was filed on behalf of two Australian and 12 Kuwaiti citizens whom the United States had captured in Afghanistan.[21] The question before the Court was whether the federal habeas statute granted jurisdiction to consider petitions brought by non-citizens located in Guantanamo. The government argued that the statute did not apply extraterritorially. The statutory text made no reference to petitioners' geographic location or citizenship.[22]

Supreme Court precedents did not necessarily decide the issue. In several cases predating the habeas statute, the Court upheld federal courts' jurisdiction over writs of habeas corpus challenging wartime detentions.[23] However, those cases typically involved persons detained in the United States.[24] In contrast, in *Johnson v. Eisentrager*,[25] a post-World War II case decided a few years after Congress enacted the current habeas statute, petitioners were serving sentences in Germany after a trial by a U.S. military commission in China. Noting six factors,[26] the Court held that the courts lacked jurisdiction over the *Eisentrager* petitions.

Writing for the five-justice majority[27] in *Rasul*, Justice Stevens relied on case-specific facts to distinguish *Eisentrager* and hold that the "[a]pplication of the habeas statute to persons detained at [Guantanamo] is consistent with the historical reach of the writ of habeas corpus."[28] To reach that conclusion, he characterized the *Eisentrager* holding as limited to its facts. He then distinguished the Guantanamo detainees from the petitioners in *Eisentrager*, concluding that the two groups "differ … in important respects."[29] In particular, he emphasized that unlike the *Eisentrager* petitioners, the Guantanamo detainees were not alien enemy combatants in a traditional conflict between state armies.[30] He also noted that unlike its detention facility in post-war Germany, the United States exercises "complete jurisdiction and control" over the Guantanamo Naval Station, pursuant to an agreement with Cuba.[31]

Justice Stevens relied on a second line of argument to support the Court's holding. He recalled *Ahrens v. Clark*,[32] a case decided a few years prior to *Eisentrager*, in which the Court interpreted the federal habeas statute as not providing jurisdiction for petitions brought by persons located outside of a court's territorial jurisdiction. (Justice Stevens was well situated to recollect that case: when the Court considered *Ahrens*, he was serving as a law clerk for Justice Rutledge, who wrote a dissenting opinion.) He then interpreted a 1973 decision as having limited *Ahrens*.[33] Particularly given the sparse precedent on the issue of the extraterritorial reach of habeas corpus rights, Justice Stevens's unique historical understanding might have been persuasive to some of the other justices.

Justice Scalia wrote a dissenting opinion in *Rasul* that rejected Justice Stevens's fact-specific distinctions in favor of a bright-line rule. He characterized *Eisentrager* as "settled law."[34] Under that precedent, he argued, courts lack jurisdiction over habeas claims brought by non-citizens outside U.S. sovereign territory.

Hamdan v. Rumsfeld

The petitioner in *Hamdan* was a Yemeni national alleged to have worked as Osama Bin Laden's bodyguard and driver. Like the petitioners in *Rasul*, he was captured in Afghanistan and detained at Guantanamo. Two years into his detention at Guantanamo, he was determined by the President to be subject to a military order establishing military commissions and charged with one count of conspiracy "to commit … offenses triable by military commission."[35] He challenged the planned military commission proceeding, arguing that (1) the Executive lacked the authority under existing statutes and the laws of war to use a military commission as the forum for a trial for the crime of conspiracy; and (2) the military commission procedures violated both the Uniform Code of Military Justice (i.e., Chapter 47 of Title 10 of the U.S. Code) and the Geneva Convention, under which he was entitled to be treated as a prisoner of war.[36]

In response, the government urged the Court to dismiss the case based on a provision of the Detainee Treatment Act that had removed federal courts' jurisdiction over habeas challenges brought by aliens held in U.S. custody as enemy combatants. The petitioner argued that the provision did not apply to cases that, like his, were pending when the measure passed, and that, in any event, it was unconstitutional.

Hamdan prompted a complicated set of opinions by the justices. Justice Stevens wrote the main majority opinion, but the opinion was divided into multiple parts, with other justices joining some but not all of them. For example, only three other justices joined a portion of Justice Stevens's opinion that held that the offense of "conspiracy ... to commit offenses triable by military commissions" was one that could not be tried by military commission.

Other parts of Justice Stevens's opinion were joined by a majority of justices and thus expressed a holding of the Court that has precedential weight. Writing for a majority of the justices, Justice Stevens rejected the argument that the Detainee Treatment Act removed federal courts' jurisdiction over Hamdan's habeas challenge.[37] That holding was grounded on an analysis of the Court's precedents regarding retroactivity of statutes, under which a presumption generally favors a prospective effect only.

Also writing for a majority, he concluded that the military commissions' procedures, as then designed, violated precepts of the Uniform Code of Military Justice (UCMJ), international laws of war incorporated into the UCMJ, and UCMJ provisions regulating military commissions. An Executive Order signed in November 2001 governed the detention and trial of non-citizens whom the President determines might have an Al Qaeda connection or might have engaged in terrorist activities directed at the United States.[38] It then provided that such individuals would be tried by military commission "for any and all offenses triable by military commissions."[39] The Court held that any power to create them must flow from the Constitution and must be among those "powers granted jointly to the President and Congress in time of war."[40] In other words, it viewed the statutes as, at most, "acknowledg[ing] a general Presidential authority to convene military commissions in circumstances where justified under the 'Constitution and laws,' including the law of war," rather than as providing an independent basis of authority for the convening of special military trials.[41] It also held that even alleged Al Qaeda members, such as Hamdan, fell within the protections of the Geneva Conventions.[42]

Justices Scalia, Thomas, and Alito wrote dissenting opinions. One point of disagreement concerned statutory interpretation. For example, Justice Scalia asserted that under the plain text of the Detainee Treatment Act, federal courts lack jurisdiction over Hamdan's habeas petition. He likewise disagreed with the majority's reading of the precedents regarding retroactivity.

Other areas of contention seemed to strike closer to the heart of separation-of-powers concerns. For instance, Justice Scalia argued that the Court should refrain from exercising jurisdiction in the case even if Congress had not prohibited its exercise, in part because of the "military exigencies" supporting the detentions and the military commission process.[43] Similarly, Justice Alito's dissenting opinion argued that the Court is bound to defer to the President's plausible interpretation of the treaty language.

ROLE IN SUBSEQUENT CASES

Because the questions regarding habeas jurisdiction were decided on statutory grounds in *Rasul* and *Hamdan*, those cases did not resolve a looming constitutional question: did the U.S. Constitution's Suspension Clause prevent Congress from stripping the federal courts of jurisdiction over Guantanamo detainees' habeas challenges? The Suspension Clause of the U.S. Constitution provides that "[t]he Privilege of the Writ of Habeas Corpus shall not be suspended, unless when in Cases of Rebellion or Invasion the public Safety may require it."[44]

After the *Hamdan* decision, Congress again enacted a statutory provision in 2006 that purported to explicitly remove federal courts' jurisdiction to review habeas challenges, including pending cases, brought by aliens held in U.S. custody as enemy combatants.[45] The constitutional question was thus prompted. A case raising the question, *Boumediene v. Bush*,[46] was soon brought.

Although Justice Stevens did not write the majority opinion in *Boumediene*, he arguably had two important roles in the case. First, when the Court earlier declined to review the case, he and Justice Kennedy issued a statement noting the "obvious importance of the issues raised" by the case, signaling a possible willingness to vote to review the case after some procedural circumstances had changed.[47] Second, as the senior Associate Justice on the Court, Justice Stevens has the role of assigning the writing of opinions in cases in which the Chief Justice is not in the majority. In *Boumediene*, Justice Stevens assigned the majority opinion to Justice Kennedy, an assignment that might have been important in retaining a five-justice majority in the case.

Justice Stevens's Legacy

Although the *Rasul* and *Hamdan* decisions were largely resolved on statutory grounds, it can be said that Justice Stevens has been instrumental in developing post-9/11 jurisprudence regarding the limits of executive power during—and following—armed conflicts. Prior to 9/11, the Supreme Court had rarely considered questions regarding potential limits on the President's Commander in Chief power.[48] The wartime detention cases provide key insights into the Court's views on the reach of executive authority, as well as on other separation-of-powers concerns, including Congress's role.

The 9/11 attacks were arguably indicative of broad and long-lasting shifts in the manner in which wars are waged. *Rasul*, *Hamdan*, and other key post-9/11 cases will likely serve as the leading line of precedents in future non-traditional conflicts. Justice Scalia and some other justices have perceived a broad vision of executive power to be well grounded in historical and legal precedents, as least where non-citizens are concerned. In contrast, Justice Stevens and other justices have viewed historical precedents as placing limits, in some circumstances, on the Executive's authority to indefinitely detain wartime captives or to set procedures for their trial. It has been asserted that Justice Stevens's jurisprudential views on such issues may have been focused, to some degree, by both his experience as a World War II veteran and his time as a law clerk for Justice Rutledge, who is said to have regretted legal interpretations he adopted to uphold the internment of Japanese Americans.[49]

Regardless, Justice Stevens's case-specific approach to such issues is likely to have both a short-term and a long-standing effect. For example, in the near future, the Court will likely review newly enacted military commission procedures, which are currently being utilized in trials of detainees. Looking into the future, the decisions are likely to impact future decisions in which the Court is called upon to decide the extent to which aliens held outside of U.S. territory are entitled to rights under the U.S. Constitution.

End Notes

[1] Authorization for Use of Military Force, P.L. 107-40 (2001). The authority also extended to those "nations, organizations, or persons" who harbored the perpetrators of the attacks.

[2] For a more in-depth examination of the Supreme Court's post-9/11 decisions regarding habeas corpus, see CRS Report RL33180, *Enemy Combatant Detainees: Habeas Corpus Challenges in Federal Court*, by Jennifer K. Elsea and Michael John Garcia.

[3] 542 U.S. 466 (2004).

[4] 548 U.S. 557 (2006).
[5] 553 U.S. 723 (2008).
[6] 542 U.S. 426 (2004).
[7] *Id.* at 455 (Stevens, J., dissenting).
[8] *Id.* at 465.
[9] *See* U.S. Const. art. I, § 9, cl. 2 ("The Privilege of the Writ of Habeas Corpus shall not be suspended, unless when in Cases of Rebellion or Invasion the public Safety may require it.").
[10] 28 U.S.C. § 2241(c)(3).
[11] Williams v. Kaiser, 323 U.S. 471, 484 n. 2 (1945).
[12] 533 U.S. 289 (2001).
[13] *Id.* at 380, n. 13.
[14] For example, a petitioner may challenge his or her custody while serving a sentence imposed after trial and appeal in the federal courts, or bring a collateral attack to challenge custody while a case or appeal is pending.
[15] *Id.*
[16] *Hamdan*, 548 U.S. at 588-89.
[17] *See, e.g.*, Daniel A. Farber, *Justice Stevens, Habeas Jurisdiction, and the War on Terror*, 43 U.C. Davis L. Rev. 945 (2009).
[18] 542 U.S. 507 (2004).
[19] A plurality of justices upheld the detention but held that the petitioner was entitled to a hearing. Justice O'Connor, writing for the plurality, stated that "a state of war is not a blank check for the President when it comes to the rights of the Nation's citizens." *Id.* at 536.
[20] *Id.* at 554 (Scalia, J., dissenting).
[21] 542 U.S. 466 (2004).
[22] *See* 28 U.S.C. § 2241 *et seq.*
[23] *See, e.g.*, Ex parte Milligan, 71 U.S. 2 (1866); Ex parte Quirin, 317 U.S. 1 (1942). *But see* In re Yamashita, 327 U.S. 1 (1946) (denying a habeas petition brought by a Japanese Army General).
[24] *But see* In re Yamashita, 327 U.S. 1 (1946) (holding that the courts had jurisdiction to review a habeas petition brought by a Japanese Army General detained in the Philippines).
[25] 339 U.S. 763 (1950).
[26] *Id.* at 777 ("To support that assumption we must hold that a prisoner of our military authorities is constitutionally entitled to the writ, even though he (a) is an enemy alien; (b) has never been or resided in the United States; (c) was captured outside of our territory and there held in military custody as a prisoner of war; (d) was tried and convicted by a Military Commission sitting outside the United States; (e) for offenses against laws of war committed outside the United States; (f) and is at all times imprisoned outside the United States.").
[27] A sixth justice, Justice Kennedy, concurred in the Court's decision.
[28] *Rasul*, 542 U.S. at 481.
[29] *Rasul*, 542 U.S. at 476.
[30] *Id.* (Noting that the Guantanamo detainees are "differently situated" because they "are not nationals of countries at war with the United States, and they deny that they have engaged in or plotted acts of aggression against the United States; they have never been afforded access to any tribunal, much less charged with and convicted of wrongdoing; and for more than two years they have been imprisoned in territory over which the United States exercises exclusive jurisdiction and control.")
[31] *See id.*; Lease of Lands for Coaling and Naval Station, Feb. 23, 1903, U.S.-Cuba, Art. III, T.S. No. 418.
[32] 335 U.S. 188 (1948).
[33] *See* Braden v. 30th Judicial Circuit Court of Ky., 410 U.S. 484, 495 (1973); *Rasul*, 542 U.S. at 478.

[34] *Id.* at 489 (Scalia, J., dissenting).

[35] *See id.* at 566 (citing App. to Pet. for Cert. 65a.).

[36] Article 5 of the Third Geneva Convention governs prisoners of war. It dictates that individuals captured during battle be treated as prisoners of war unless they are determined to be unlawful enemy combatants.

[37] *Hamdan*, 548 U.S. at 583-584.

[38] Detention, Treatment, and Trial of Certain Non-Citizens in the War Against Terrorism, 66 Fed. Reg. 57833 (Nov. 13, 2001).

[39] *Id.*

[40] *Hamdan*, 548 U.S. at 591 (citing Congress's powers to "declare War ... and make Rules concerning Captures on Land and Water," Art. I, § 8, cl. 11, to "raise and support Armies," *Id.*, cl. 12, to "define and punish ... Offences against the Law of Nations," *Id.*, cl. 10, and "To make Rules for the Government and Regulation of the land and naval Forces," *Id.*, cl. 14.).

[41] *Hamdan*, 548 U.S. at 594-595.

[42] *Id.* at 630.

[43] *See id.* at 673-73 (Scalia, J., dissenting).

[44] U.S. Const. art. I, § 9, cl. 2.

[45] Military Commissions Act of 2006, P.L. 109-366, § 7.

[46] 553 U.S. 723 (2008).

[47] Boumediene v. Bush, 549 U.S. 1328 (2007).

[48] Perhaps the leading Supreme Court opinion on that issue is Justice Robert Jackson's concurring opinion in a Korean War era case, Youngstown Steel & Tube Co., 343 U.S. 579 (1952). *See also Hamdan*, 548 U.S. at 638 ("The proper framework for assessing whether executive actions are authorized is the three-part scheme used by Justice Jackson in his opinion in Youngstown."). Justice Jackson's framework was invoked in both majority and dissenting opinions after 9/11, with justices reaching differing conclusions.

[49] *See, e.g.*, Deborah Pearlstein, *The Path from Chevron to Hamdan: Justice Stevens and National Security Cases*, Apr. 21, 2010, http://www.scotusblog.com/2010/04/the-path-from-chevron-to-hamdan/#more-19018.

In: Jurisprudence of Supreme Court Justice... ISBN: 978-1-61761-282-4
Editor: Harvey B. Lymont

Chapter 5

JUSTICE STEVENS: DEATH PENALTY JURISPRUDENCE

Todd Garvey

SUMMARY

Justice Stevens's position on the death penalty has transformed during his tenure on the Court. Although Stevens initially supported the imposition of the death penalty in accordance with adequately protective state enacted guidelines, over the next 35 years the Justice has voted to narrow the application of the death penalty as he has become more skeptical of the punishment's underlying rationale and the states' ability to protect the rights of capital defendants. In 2008, Justice Stevens questioned the continuing constitutionality of the death penalty in his concurring opinion in *Baze v. Rees*.[1]

Shortly before Justice Stevens's appointment, the U.S. Supreme Court, in *Furman v. Georgia*, established what amounted to a moratorium on the imposition of the death penalty.[2] The 1972 decision invalidated the capital punishment systems of Georgia and Texas along with the systems of "no less than 39 states and the District of Columbia," holding that the inherently arbitrary and discriminatory nature of the states' application of the death penalty violated both the prohibition against cruel and unusual punishment of the Eighth Amendment and the due process guarantees of the Fourteenth

Amendment.[3] Following the *Furman* case, capital punishment essentially ceased to exist anywhere in the United States.

However, less than six months after Justice Stevens took his seat on the Supreme Court, and four years after *Furman*, Stevens cast an essential, if not deciding,[4] vote in favor of reviving the death penalty. In the *Gregg* cases, the Supreme Court, in a series of decisions, upheld a number of reenacted state capital punishment schemes that had been tailored to remedying the constitutional deficiencies identified in *Furman*.[5] *Gregg*, and its companion cases issued that same day, have been characterized as representing the "resurrection" of capital punishment.[6] At the time, Justice Stevens had confidence that the states could indeed provide adequate procedural safeguards— with guidance from a continued re-examination of capital sentencing procedures by the Court— that would successfully eliminate the constitutional concerns associated with the states' earlier use of the death penalty.[7]

JUSTICE STEVENS'S "NARROWING JURISPRUDENCE"

In the decades following *Gregg*, Justice Stevens's death penalty jurisprudence was governed by his belief in "fundamental fairness" and the notion that the death penalty, as the ultimate punishment, must be treated differently from any other lesser form of punishment.[8] The "qualitative difference" between death and any other form of punishment, wrote Justice Stevens, leads to a "corresponding difference in the need for reliability in the determination that death is the appropriate punishment in a specific case."[9]

In case after case, Stevens has voted to narrow the application of the death penalty through limiting the class of individuals that was eligible for the punishment, or by increasing procedural protections for capital defendants. Justice Stevens, often in dissent, has voted to prohibit judges from overriding a jury's decision on the imposition of the death penalty;[10] limit the use of emotional victim impact statements;[11] ensure adequate legal representation for capital defendants;[12] prohibit the use of the death penalty on the mentally retarded;[13] prohibit the use of the death penalty on minors;[14] alter the composition of jury pools in capital cases to include those who object on moral grounds to the imposition of the death penalty;[15] prohibit substantially delayed executions;[16] overturn convictions that "present an unacceptable risk that race played a decisive role in [the defendant's] sentencing";[17] and prohibit states from punishing the crime of rape, or rape of a child, with the death penalty.[18] Perhaps the opinion that is most representative of Justice Stevens's attempts at narrowing the application of the death penalty, and one in which Stevens was able to draw five other justices to his position, was his majority opinion in the 2002 case *Atkins v. Virginia*.[19]

Atkins v. Virginia: A National Consensus

A landmark case, *Atkins v. Virginia* highlights two key aspects of Justice Stevens's death penalty jurisprudence. The opinion illustrates the Justice's reliance on state-by-state trends in assessing societal views on what qualifies as "cruel and unusual."[20] Additionally, the opinion discusses Stevens's growing skepticism of the accepted justifications for capital punishment.

In *Atkins*, the Court considered the constitutionality of imposing the death penalty on the mentally retarded.[21] The mentally retarded defendant in the case had been found guilty of abduction, armed robbery, and capital murder and sentenced to death by a jury under Virginia law.[22] Writing for the majority, Justice Stevens overturned the sentence on the grounds that the punishment was disproportionate to the crime and therefore in violation of the prohibition on cruel and unusual punishment of the Eighth Amendment.[23]

Justice Stevens began by summarizing the Court's Eighth Amendment jurisprudence, noting that at its core, the amendment's prohibition on excessive punishment demands that "punishment for crime should be graduated and proportioned to the offense."[24] Known as the proportionality principle, whether a punishment is excessive in relation to the crime is judged not by the views that prevailed when the Bill of Rights was adopted, but by the "evolving standards of decency that mark the progress of a maturing society."[25] Stevens went on to cite long-standing Court precedent in concluding that the "clearest and most reliable objective evidence of contemporary values is the legislation enacted by the country's legislature."[26] The Court, both before and after *Atkins*, has utilized the actions of the state legislatures as a barometer of society's acceptance of the death penalty in a given scenario.[27]

In considering how state legislatures have approached the issue of imposing the death penalty on the mentally retarded, Justice Stevens identified a clear trend towards prohibiting the practice. Although a majority of states had not yet prohibited the use of capital punishment on the mentally retarded, Stevens noted "it is not so much the number of these states that is significant, but the consistency of the direction of change."[28] After showing the clear trend among the states towards prohibiting the practice over the previous decade, Stevens concluded that imposing the death penalty on the mentally retarded had "become truly unusual, and it is fair to say that a national consensus has developed against it."[29] As a Justice, Stevens typically placed greater weight on current trends, rather than simply deferring to the position adopted by a majority of state legislatures.[30]

Stevens's opinion also determined that the social purposes served by the death penalty— retribution and deterrence—were not adequate to justify the execution of a mentally retarded criminal. Retribution, argued Stevens, is directly associated with culpability. As the "severity of the appropriate punishment necessarily depends on the culpability of the defendant," the Court has reserved the imposition of the death penalty for only the most serious crimes and the most culpable defendants.[31] Stevens concluded that the lesser degree of culpability, due to cognitive and behavioral impairments associated with the mentally retarded defendant, "surely does not merit that form of retribution."[32] As to deterrence, Stevens noted that the diminished ability of the mentally retarded to "engage in logical reasoning, or to control impulses," defeated the purpose of creating a deterrent as it was less likely that mentally retarded individuals could "process the information of the possibility of execution as a penalty and, as a result, control their conduct based upon that information."[33]

Stevens then concisely summarized his "narrowing" view of the death penalty, developed over more than 30 years of experience on the Court, in concluding: "[T]hus pursuant to our narrowing jurisprudence, which seeks to ensure that only the most deserving of execution are put to death, an exclusion for the mentally retarded is appropriate."[34]

THE CULMINATION OF JUSTICE STEVENS'S EVOLVING DEATH PENALTY JURISPRUDENCE

In 2008, Justice Stevens abandoned his three-decade endeavor of attaining a narrowed, fair, and non-discriminatory capital punishment system. Rather, Stevens's position on the death penalty came full circle in *Baze v. Rees* as he cited back to the Court's decision in *Furman* in asserting that capital punishment was "patently excessive and cruel and unusual punishment violative of the Eighth Amendment."[35]

In *Baze*, the Court heard an Eighth Amendment challenge to Kentucky's multi-drug lethal injection procedure. [36] Although a majority of the Court voted to uphold Kentucky's method of execution, including Justice Stevens, it was Stevens's concurring opinion that drew the most attention. Picking up where he left off in *Atkins*, Stevens questioned the accepted rationales underlying the death penalty.[37] His opinion openly attacked the legitimacy of the deterrence and retribution rationales, arguing that the value of both had dwindled and must now be "called into question."[38] With respect to deterrence, Stevens noted that "despite 30 years of empirical research in the area, there remains no reliable statistical evidence that capital punishment in fact deters potential offenders."[39] As to retribution, he pointed out that the relatively painless methods of execution required under the Eighth Amendment "actually undermine the very premise on which public approval of the retribution rationale is based"—that the offender suffer a punishment comparable to the suffering experienced by his victim.[40]

In confronting the Court's decisions, and his vote in the *Gregg* cases, Justice Stevens admitted that the Court "relied heavily on our belief that adequate procedures were in place that would avoid the danger of discriminatory application identified ... in *Furman*."[41] Stevens then pointed to three key failures of the Court's death penalty jurisprudence. First, juries in capital cases do not represent a fair cross section of the community; rather, eliminating jurors who oppose the death penalty on moral grounds "is really a procedure that has the purpose and effect of obtaining a jury that is biased in favor of conviction."[42] Second, the emotional impact of capital offenses and the often disturbing facts associated with those crimes leads to a greater risk of error in capital cases because "the interest in making sure the crime does not go unpunished may overcome residual doubt concerning the identity of the offender."[43] Third, Justice Stevens highlighted the continued risk of a discriminatory application of the death penalty, noting that the Court has continued to allow race to play an "unacceptable role" in capital cases.[44]

Given what he considered the now unpersuasive rationales for the death penalty, and the inability of the Court and the states to cooperatively establish adequate procedural protections in capital cases, Justice Stevens, relying on his "own experience" and "extensive exposure" to death penalty cases, quoted the Court's decision in *Furman* in unequivocally concluding that the death penalty represents "the pointless and needless extinction of life with only marginal contributions to any discernible social or public purpose. A penalty with such negligible returns to the state is patently excessive and cruel and unusual punishment violative of the Eighth Amendment."[45]

Notwithstanding his clear position that the death penalty itself was unconstitutional, Stevens voted to uphold the Kentucky lethal injection statute. Citing a "respect [for] precedents that remain a part of our law," Stevens deferred to the Court's long-standing framework for evaluating the death penalty in light of the Eighth Amendment, and joined the Court in concluding that, under the existing framework, the evidence failed to show that the Kentucky statute was unconstitutional.[46]

STEVENS'S LEGACY

From casting a vote that resurrected the use of the death penalty to becoming the only Justice thus far on the Roberts Court to formally question the death penalty's *per se* constitutionality, Justice Stevens's position on capital punishment has undergone significant changes during his tenure on the Court. However, his jurisprudence has been consistently guided by his belief in "fundamental fairness" and his recognition that, due to its special risks and irrevocable nature, "death is different." Although Stevens initially had hopes that the Court, working in cooperation with the states, could correct the imperfections of capital punishment, after more than 30 years of experience with death penalty cases, and a declining acceptance of the proffered justifications for the death penalty, Justice Stevens ultimately has questioned whether sentencing a defendant to death can ever be consistent with the Eighth Amendment's prohibition on "cruel and unusual" punishment. With his retirement imminent, the Court faces the loss of its most vocal death penalty opponent.

End Notes

[1] 553 U.S. 35 (2008) (Stevens, J., concurring).
[2] 408 U.S. 238 (1972).
[3] *Id.* at 417-18.
[4] Elisabeth Semel, *Reflection on Justice John Paul Stevens's Concurring Opinion in Baze v. Rees: A Fifth Gregg Justice Renounces Capital Punishment*, 43 U.C. Davis L. Rev. 783, 787 (2010) ("[Justice Stevens's] vote was indispensable to the Court's revival of the death penalty in 1976.").
[5] 428 U.S. 153 (1976); Jurek v. Texas, 428 U.S. 262 (1976); Proffitt v. Florida 428 U.S. 242 (1976).
[6] Semel, *supra* note 4, *citing* Stuart Banner, The Death Penalty: An American History 267 (2002).

[7] Gardner v. Florida, 430 U.S. 349, 357 (1977).

[8] William W. Berry III, *Powell, Blackmun, Stevens, and the Pandora's Box theory of Judicial Restraint*, *available at* http://www.ssrn.com; *see. e.g.*, Jacobs v. Scott 513 U.S. 1067, 1067 (1994) ("In my opinion it is fundamentally unfair ...").

[9] McClesky v. Kemp, 481 U.S. 279, 366 (1987) (Stevens, J., dissenting). Justice Stevens recently reiterated that his concern over wrongful convictions has played a role in shaping his views on the death penalty, noting that "the risk of an incorrect decision has increased" and that DNA testing makes us "more aware of the risk [of wrongful conviction] than we might have been before." Joan Biskupic, *Stevens, Risk of Wrongful Sentences Higher*, USA Today, May, 6 2010.

[10] Spaziano v. Florida, 468 U.S. 447 (1984) (Stevens, J., concurring in part and dissenting in part).

[11] Payne v. Tennessee, 501 U.S. 808 (1991) (Stevens, J., dissenting)

[12] Lockhart v. Fretwell, 506 U.S. 364 (1993).

[13] Atkins v. Virginia, 536 U.S. 304 (2002).

[14] Roper v. Simmons, 543 U.S. 551 (2005) (Stevens, J., concurring).

[15] *See*, Baze v. Rees, 553 U.S. 35 (2008) (Stevens, J., concurring).

[16] *See*, Thompson v. McNeil, 129 S. Ct 1299 (2009).

[17] McClesky v. Kemp, 481 U.S. 279 (1987) (Stevens, J., dissenting).

[18] Coker v. Georgia, 433 U.S. 584 (1977); Kennedy v. Louisiana, 128 S.Ct. 2641 (2008).

[19] 536 U.S. 304 (2002).

[20] *Id.* at 312-316.

[21] *Id.* at 306.

[22] *Id.* at 307.

[23] *Id.* at 321.

[24] *Id.* at 311 (quoting Weems v. U.S., 217 U.S. 349, 367 (1910)).

[25] *Id.* at 312 (quoting Trop v. Dulles, 356 U.S. 86, 100-01 (1958)).

[26] *Id.* at 312.

[27] *See*, Penry v. Lynaugh, 492 U.S. 302, 331 (1989) (stating that "the clearest and most reliable objective evidence of contemporary values is the legislation enacted by the country's legislatures."); Roper v. Simmons, 543 U.S. 551, 568 (2005) ("A majority of States have rejected the imposition of the death penalty on juvenile offenders under 18 ..."). *See also*, Kennedy v. Louisiana, 128 S.Ct. 2641 (2008).

[28] *Atkins*, 536 U.S. at 315.

[29] *Id.* at 316.

[30] For example, Justice Stevens voted to prohibit the use of the death penalty on juveniles even though a majority of states allowed the practice. *Roper*, 543 U.S. 551 (2005).

[31] *Atkins*, 536 U.S. at 319.

[32] *Id.*

[33] *Id.* at 320.

[34] *Id.* at 319.

[35] 553 U.S. 35, 86 (2008) (Stevens, J., concurring).

[36] *Id.* at 40.

[37] *Id.* at 78-82.

[38] *Id.* at 78.

[39] *Id.* at 79.

[40] *Id.* at 81.

[41] *Id.* at 83.

[42] *Id.* at 84.

[43] *Id.* at 84-5.

[44] *Id.* at 85.

[45] *Id.* at 86 (quoting Furman v. Georgia, 408 U.S. 238, 312 (1972) (White, J., concurring)).

[46] *Id.* at 87.

In: Jurisprudence of Supreme Court Justice... ISBN: 978-1-61761-282-4
Editor: Harvey B. Lymont

Chapter 6

THE JURISPRUDENCE OF JUSTICE JOHN PAUL STEVENS: SELECTED OPINIONS ON THE JURY'S ROLE IN CRIMINAL SENTENCING

Anna C. Henning

SUMMARY

Justice Stevens has played a critical role in the Supreme Court's interpretation of a jury's role in criminal sentencing. In 2000, he wrote the majority opinion for the Court in *Apprendi v. New Jersey*, a landmark case in which the Court held that a judge typically may not increase a sentence beyond the range prescribed by statute unless the increase is based on facts determined by a jury "beyond a reasonable doubt." In 2005, he wrote one of two majority opinions in *United States v. Booker*, in which the Court applied the *Apprendi* rule to the Federal Sentencing Guidelines. In those two cases and in several other cases on this issue during the past few decades, Justice Stevens has been a leading voice, articulating a broad interpretation of the jury trial and due process rights at issue.

INTRODUCTION

Justice Stevens has been a key figure in the Supreme Court's recent decisions interpreting the scope of two "companion rights":[1] the due process right to a "beyond a reasonable doubt" determination and the right to trial by jury. The right to a jury trial in criminal prosecutions is explicitly protected in the Sixth Amendment to the U.S. Constitution.[2] The "proof beyond a reasonable doubt" standard is guaranteed by the Due Process Clauses of the Fifth Amendment (federal proceedings) and the Fourteenth Amendment (state proceedings).[3] Together, those constitutional provisions require that a criminal conviction follow a jury determination of "proof beyond a reasonable doubt of every fact necessary to constitute the crime."[4]

Those rights have a strong legal and historical foundation. However, a question emerged regarding their application to sentencing determinations, particularly as "sentence enhancements" became a popular legislative tool: to what extent do facts taken into account during sentencing require a "beyond a reasonable doubt" determination by a jury?

Justice Stevens has had a critical role in the Supreme Court's resolution of that question, in several respects. First, he asserted that the constitutional question should be addressed, describing the constitutional guarantees at issue as being of "surpassing importance."[5] Second, along with Justice Scalia, in early cases reviewing sentencing enhancements, he indicated his broad interpretation of the jury trial and due process rights. In a concurring opinion, for example, he wrote, "I am convinced that it is unconstitutional for a legislature to remove from the jury the assessment of facts that increase the prescribed range of penalties to which a criminal defendant is exposed." He added that "[i]t is equally clear that such facts must be established by proof beyond a reasonable doubt."[6] Third, having persuaded five of the Court's nine justices of his views, he authored the opinion for the Court in a *Apprendi v. New Jersey*,[7] the leading case in which the Court announced a broad reading of the constitutional rights at issue. Finally, he wrote for the Court in *United States v. Booker*,[8] a decision applying the *Apprendi* holding to the Federal Sentencing Guidelines.

Although this line of cases has resulted in closely divided opinions, the justices were not divided along typical lines. Justice Scalia has been the other justice arguing in agreement with Justice Stevens in many of the cases addressing a jury's role in criminal sentencing. In *Apprendi*, Justices Scalia, Thomas, Souter, and Ginsburg joined Justice Stevens's majority opinion.

PRE-*APPRENDI* CASES

Justice Stevens's opinion in *Apprendi* was foreshadowed in several dissenting and concurring opinions in cases decided during the 1980s and 1990s. The first such case was *McMillan v. Pennsylvania*,[9] decided in 1986. *McMillan* involved a Pennsylvania statute establishing a mandatory five-year minimum prison sentence in cases in which a judge finds, by a preponderance of the evidence (a lower standard than "beyond a reasonable doubt"), that the defendant visibly possessed a firearm during the commission of the offense. The statute expressly stated that the firearm possession "shall not be an element of the crime."[10] Instead, it stated that it "shall be determined at sentencing," indicating that it was to be removed from typical jury trial and "beyond a reasonable doubt" requirements.[11] The U.S. Supreme Court upheld the statute. Writing for the Court, Chief Justice Rehnquist emphasized that the state legislature expressly designated firearm possession as a "sentencing factor," rather than "an element of the crime." The Court concluded that the state legislature had intended to create a sentencing factor which "operates solely to limit the sentencing court's discretion in selecting a penalty within the range already available to it."[12]

Justice Stevens wrote a dissenting opinion, not joined by any other justice, in which he first articulated his view of the constitutional implications of sentencing statutes of this kind. "In my view," he wrote, "a state legislature may not dispense with the requirement of proof beyond a reasonable doubt for conduct that it targets for severe criminal penalties."[13] His disagreement with the Court stemmed in part from his interpretation of prior precedents. He agreed with the statement from a prior case, also quoted by the majority, that "[the] applicability of the reasonable-doubt standard ... has always been dependent on how a State defines the offense that is charged."[14] However, he interpreted that holding to ensure that states have discretion regarding what conduct to criminalize, not over which conduct will be treated as a "criminal element" versus a "sentencing factor."[15] "In my opinion," he concluded, "the constitutional significance of the special sanction cannot be avoided by the cavalier observation that it merely 'ups the ante' for the defendant."[16]

A 1998 case, *Almendarez-Torres v. United States*,[17] involved a federal statute that makes it a crime to, among other things, return to the United States (without express consent of the Attorney General) after having been deported.[18] A general provision authorizes criminal penalties of up to two years imprisonment.[19] A second provision authorizes greater penalties in cases in which the alien was removed after a conviction for one of several specified crimes.[20] In *Almendarez-Torres*, the defendant had been deported subsequent to three convictions for aggravated felonies, for which the statute increased the maximum prison sentence for reentry to 20 years. Prosecutors did not introduce the fact of the aggravated felonies at the indictment or trial phase. Nevertheless, at sentencing, the U.S. district court relied on those aggravated felony convictions to enhance the sentence.

A five-justice majority on the Supreme Court framed the question on appeal as "whether [the aggravated felony provision] defines a separate crime or simply authorizes an enhanced penalty."[21] Noting that the provision's concern is recidivism—a factor commonly weighed in sentencing decisions, it held that it is "reasonably clear" that Congress intended to "set forth a sentencing factor" rather than a "separate crime."[22] Thus, it concluded that the statute "simply authorizes a court to increase the sentence," and thus does not require a determination by a jury.[23]

Justice Stevens and two other justices joined a dissent written by Justice Scalia. Justice Scalia asserted that the Court's prior decisions made it "genuinely doubtful whether the Constitution permits a judge (rather than a jury) to determine by a mere preponderance of the evidence (rather than beyond a reasonable doubt) a fact that increases the maximum penalty to which a criminal defendant is subject."[24]

Justice Stevens wrote an opinion reiterating his view on the constitutional question the following year, in *Jones v. United States*.[25] The defendant in *Jones* was convicted for violation of a federal carjacking statute, 18 U.S.C. § 2119. That statute generally caps imprisonment for violations at 15 years, but a subsection increased the maximum prison term in cases in which "serious bodily injury ... results." The defendant, Nathaniel Jones, was charged with carjacking, but the specific allegation that the carjacking resulted in serious bodily injury was not raised until the sentencing phase. At that time, the court found that serious bodily injury had occurred and increased Jones's sentence accordingly. No jury determinations were made on that question. The Court resolved the case on statutory grounds. In an opinion by Justice Souter, it held that the "serious bodily injury" prong, as written in the existing statute, constituted a separate criminal offense, and thus needed to be determined by a jury "beyond a reasonable doubt." It indicated that a different reading of the statute might "raise serious constitutional questions," but avoided resolving such issues because the case could be resolved on statutory grounds.[26]

In brief concurring opinions in *Jones*, Justices Stevens made clear that he would have reached the constitutional issues lurking in the case.[27] Furthermore, he expressed the view that "it is unconstitutional to remove from the jury the assessment of facts that increase the prescribed range of penalties to which a criminal defendant is exposed."[28]

APPRENDI V. NEW JERSEY

Justice Stevens expressed that view on behalf of the Court in *Apprendi v. New Jersey*.[29] In *Apprendi*, the Court reviewed a New Jersey statute that authorized 10- to 20-year increases in prison sentences if a defendant's actions were found by a judge, by a preponderance of the evidence, to have been committed with a purpose to intimidate the victim because of the victim's race or other specified characteristics. The defendant, Charles Apprendi, was found to have fired a gun into the home of an African American family. The morning of his arrest, he was alleged to have stated that "because [the family is] black in color he does not want them in the neighborhood." He later argued that his statements had been mischaracterized.[30]

In the state prosecution, Apprendi pleaded guilty to three weapon possession charges. In the plea agreement, the state reserved the right to request a sentencing enhancement based on the state's "hate crimes" statute.[31] At sentencing, evidence was presented to support and refute Apprendi's alleged racial motivation in firing into the victims' home.[32] Applying a preponderance of the evidence standard as directed by the state statute, the state trial judge concluded that Apprendi had acted with racial prejudice and accordingly enhanced his sentence on that basis.

On appeal, Apprendi argued that the Fifth and Fourteenth Amendment Due Process Clauses require that the facts justifying the sentence enhancement (i.e., a motivation of prejudice) to be found by a jury using the "beyond a reasonable doubt" standard. Both a state appellate court and the New Jersey Supreme Court rejected Apprendi's argument.[33] Relying in part on the U.S. Supreme Court's rulings in *Almendarez-Torres* and *McMillan v. Pennsylvania*, they held that the "biased purpose" determination was not an element of the underlying offense and thus did not require a jury finding of proof beyond a reasonable doubt.

The U.S. Supreme Court reversed. Writing for the Court, Justice Stevens asserted that the constitutional question was "starkly presented" by the facts in the case.[34] He examined the history of the constitutional rights involved, noting that statutory sentence enhancements are a relatively new development in a landscape of constitutional rights with centuries-old foundations. He acknowledged that the history supports judges' ability to exercise discretion in sentencing. However, he argued that such discretion has generally been limited to determinations regarding an appropriate sentence within a given range; it has not historically been extended to authorize additional penalties on the basis of a new factual determination.[35] After reviewing the history and relevant precedents, he articulated the Court's major holding: "Other than the fact of a prior conviction, any fact that increases the penalty for a crime beyond the prescribed statutory maximum must be submitted to a jury, and proved beyond a reasonable doubt."[36]

APPLYING *APPRENDI* TO SENTENCING GUIDELINES

Key cases decided after *Apprendi* have addressed the decision's application to sentencing guidelines. In a 2004 case, *Blakely* v. *Washington*,[37] the defendant challenged a sentence imposed pursuant to Washington State's sentencing guidelines. He was convicted of a crime for which the guidelines designated a maximum sentence of 53 months imprisonment, but was sentenced to 90 months after the sentencing judge found that he had acted with "deliberate cruelty"—a factor for which the guidelines authorized judges to increase a sentence. In an opinion written by Justice Scalia and joined by Justice Stevens and three other justices, the Supreme Court applied *Apprendi* to strike down the sentencing scheme. It held that the "statutory maximum" for *App rendi* purposes is the maximum sentence a judge may impose solely on the basis of the facts reflected in the jury verdict or admitted by the defendant.[38]

One year later, Justice Stevens wrote one of two majority opinions[39] for the Court in *United States v. Booker*,[40] in which the Court addressed the question whether the *Blakely* holding applied to the Federal Sentencing Guidelines. The case involved a conviction for possession with intent to distribute crack cocaine. At sentencing, the judge found, by a preponderance of the evidence, that the defendant had distributed additional drugs and obstructed justice, and increased the sentence on that basis. Applying *Apprendi* and *Blakely*, the Court held that "[a]ny fact (other than a prior conviction) which is necessary to support a sentence exceeding the maximum authorized by the facts established by a plea of guilty or a jury verdict must be admitted by the defendant or proved to a jury beyond a reasonable doubt."[41] Justice Stevens characterized the holding as a reaffirmation of the *Apprendi* holding.[42]

His opinion again emphasized the historical importance of the constitutional rights at issue.[43]

A different majority of justices joined an opinion written by Justice Breyer. In that opinion, the Court interpreted the constitutional holding (announced in the opinion by Justice Stevens) as requiring the Court to strike down two provisions of the Federal Sentencing Act,[44] including one which made the guidelines mandatory.[45] That holding was based on the Court's determination of what Congress might have intended in light of the Court's constitutional holding. It concluded that Congress would not have intended the guidelines to be made mandatory in situations where a judge is constitutionally required to receive jury determinations regarding facts relevant to sentencing.

Justice Stevens dissented from that opinion. He characterized the Court's invalidation of the Sentencing Act provisions as judicial overstepping, arguing that the constitutional holding in the case "does not authorize the Court's creative remedy" with regard to the Federal Sentencing Act.[46] He asserted that "[b]ecause the Guidelines as written possess the virtue of combining a mandatory determination of sentencing ranges and discretionary decisions within those ranges, they allow ample latitude for judicial factfinding that does not even arguably raise any Sixth Amendment issue."[47]

CONCLUSION

The impact of Justice Stevens's role, and of the *Apprendi* case in particular, has been to limit the extent to which criminal penalties can be increased based on facts found by a judge rather than a jury. Although it remains permissible for judges to take relevant facts into consideration when rendering criminal sentences, they now may not increase sentences beyond the prescribed statutory maximum unless the facts supporting such an increase are found by a jury beyond a reasonable doubt. As can be seen in the cases applying that holding to sentencing guidelines, Justice Stevens's interpretation of the constitutional trial-by-jury and due process rights has had practical and lasting effects on criminal sentencing.

End Notes

[1] *See* Apprendi v. New Jersey, 530 U.S. 466, 478 (2000) (referring to the proof beyond a reasonable doubt standard as a "companion right" to the right to a trial by jury).

[2] U.S. Const. amend. VI ("In all criminal prosecutions, the accused shall enjoy the right to a ... trial, by an impartial jury"). The Sixth Amendment jury requirement applies to state prosecutions by virtue of that amendment's incorporation in the Due Process Clause of the Fourteenth Amendment. *See* Duncan v. Louisiana, 391 U.S. 145 (1968).

[3] U.S. Const. amend. V ("No person shall ... be deprived of life, liberty, or property, without due process of law...."); U.S. Const. amend. XIV ("No state shall ... deprive any person of life, liberty, or property, without due process of law....").

[4] In re Winship, 397 U.S. 358, 364 (1970). *See also* United States v. Gaudin, 515 U.S. 506, 510 (1995) ("[The Due Process Clause and the Sixth Amendment] require criminal convictions to rest upon a jury determination that the defendant is guilty of every element of the crime with which he is charged, beyond a reasonable doubt.") (citing Sullivan v. Louisiana, 508 U.S. 275, 277-278 (1993)).

[5] *Apprendi*, 530 U.S. at 476.

[6] *See, e.g.*, Jones v. United States, 526 U.S. 227, 252-53 (1999) (Stevens, J., concurring).

[7] 530 U.S. 466 (2000).

[8] 543 U:S. 220 (2005).

[9] 477 U.S. 79 (1986).

[10] 42 Pa. Const. Stat. § 9712 (1982).

[11] *Id.*

[12] *McMillan*, 477 U.S. at 88.

[13] *Id.* at 96.

[14] *Id.* at 85 (quoting Patterson v. New York, 432 U.S. 197, 211 n. 12 (1977)); *Id.* at 98 (Stevens, J., dissenting).

[15] *Id.* at 98.

[16] *Id.* at 104.

[17] 523 U.S. 224 (1998).

[18] 8 U.S.C. § 1326.

[19] 8 U.S.C. § 1326(a).

[20] 8 U.S.C. § 1326(b).

[21] *Almendarez-Torres*, 523 U.S. at 226.

[22] *Id.* at 230.

[23] *Id.* at 226-27.

[24] *Id.* at 251 (Scalia, J., dissenting). Although the conclusion articulated by Justice Scalia now generally represents the Court's approach, the fact of a prior conviction has been treated differently. *See Apprendi*, 530 U.S. at 489 (carving an exception for a judge's taking account of prior convictions during sentencing).

[25] 526 U.S. 227 (1999).

[26] *Id.* at 251-52.

[27] Justice Scalia also wrote a short concurring opinion in *Jones*, in which he expressed views similar to Stevens's approach. *See id.* at 253 (Scalia, J., concurring).

[28] *Id.* at 252 (Stevens, J., concurring).

[29] 530 U.S. 466 (2000).

[30] *Id.* at 469-70.

[31] In its opinion, the New Jersey Supreme Court referred to the statute as one that provided a "hate crime" sentencing enhancement. The U.S. Supreme Court instead referred to the enhancement as a "biased purpose enhancement."

[32] Apprendi presented seven character witnesses and a psychologist to refute the allegations of racial bias. *Apprendi*, 530 U.S. at 470-71.

[33] State v. Apprendi, 698 A.2d 1265 (N.J. Super. Ct. App. Div. 1997), *aff'd* 731 A.2d 485 (N.J. 1999).

[34] *Apprendi*, 530 U.S. at 476.

[35] *Id.* at 481.

[36] *Id.* at 489.

[37] 542 U.S. 296 (2004).

[38] *Id.* at 302.

[39] *Booker* resulted in a complicated breakdown of opinions, with Justices Scalia, Souter, Thomas, and Ginsburg joining Justice Stevens's majority opinion resolving the constitutional issue, and another set of justices (Rehnquist, O'Connor, Kennedy, Breyer, and Ginsburg) joining to form a majority regarding the constitutional holding's impact on the guidelines.

[40] 543 U.S. 220 (2005).

[41] *Id.* at 244.

[42] *Id.*

[43] *See, e.g., id.* at 237 (stating that the "new sentencing practice forced the Court to address the question of how the right of jury trial could be preserved, in a meaningful way guaranteeing that the jury would still stand between the individual and the power of the government under the new sentencing regime.").

[44] 18 U.S.C. § 3551 *et seq.*; 28 U.S.C. § 991 *et seq.*

[45] *Booker*, 543 U.S. at 245, 259.

[46] *Id.* at 272 (Stevens, J., dissenting).

[47] *Id.* at 273.

In: Jurisprudence of Supreme Court Justice... ISBN: 978-1-61761-282-4
Editor: Harvey B. Lymont

Chapter 7

THE JURISPRUDENCE OF JUSTICE JOHN PAUL STEVENS: THE *CHEVRON* DOCTRINE

Todd Garvey

SUMMARY

One of Justice John Paul Stevens's most lasting jurisprudential legacies is his opinion in *Chevron v. Natural Resources Defense Council*. The 1984 case, a landmark decision in both administrative law and separation of powers, established the legal framework that has largely governed the degree of deference a court will accord a federal agency in interpreting and implementing statutes. What began as an unexceptional case focusing on the meaning of the phrase "stationary source" in the Clean Air Act has developed into one of the most frequently cited cases ever. Although often relied on as an authority, the case has also engendered significant confusion. Questions of when, and how, to apply the two-step *Chevron* analysis laid out by Justice Stevens, which is simple in theory yet remarkably varied in its application, have consistently challenged federal judges. Moreover, although Justice Stevens has spent the last quarter century working to clarify the *Chevron* doctrine, as he departs the Court he may find himself outside the majority position on at least one key aspect of the test's application.

Stevens's *Chevron* analysis established what many commentators have considered to be a highly deferential judicial role when faced with a challenge to an agency's interpretation of its own authorizing statute or a statute it administers. At step one of the analysis, a reviewing court must determine whether Congress has spoken clearly on the issue at hand and give effect to any intent it finds Congress expressed unambiguously. An agency interpretation that is contrary to the clear intent of Congress must be rejected. If, however, Congress's intent is unclear as to the immediate question, including where Congress is silent, at step two the court's role is to defer to any reasonable agency interpretation of the pertinent statutory language. This analysis is commonly referred to as the *Chevron* "two-step."

As much as Justice Stevens's opinion has been cited, major questions remain about when and how to properly apply the *Chevron* test. The threshold question of what types of agency interpretations qualify for *Chevron* deference, for example, has narrowed. A second ongoing dispute, and one in which Justice Stevens has played a leading role, relates to what tools of statutory construction are properly employed at step one of the test as a court determines Congress's "intent." Specifically, should the court be considering legislative intent and legislative purpose or restrict itself to the statutory language alone?

INTRODUCTION

One of Justice Stevens's most lasting jurisprudential legacies is his opinion in *Chevron v. Natural Resources Defense Council.*[1] The 1984 case, a landmark decision in both administrative law and separation of powers, established the legal framework that has largely governed the degree of deference a court will accord a federal agency in interpreting and implementing statutes. What began as an unexceptional case focusing on the meaning of the phrase "stationary source" in the Clean Air Act has developed into one of the most frequently cited cases ever.[2] Although often relied on as an authority, the case has also engendered significant confusion. Questions of when, and how, to apply the two-step *Chevron* analysis laid out by Justice Stevens, which is simple in theory yet remarkably varied in its application, have consistently challenged federal judges. Moreover, although Justice Stevens has spent the last quarter century working to clarify the *Chevron* doctrine, as he departs the Court he may find himself outside the majority position on at least one key aspect of the test's application.

This chapter will detail the *Chevron* decision, describe the two-part test laid out by Justice Stevens for determining whether to accord deference to an agency interpretation, and discuss the rationales underlying that judicial deference. Finally, the chapter will consider the significant influence the opinion has had within administrative law, while highlighting a number of unresolved questions relating to the proper application of the *Chevron* test.

THE *CHEVRON* DECISION

The facts of the *Chevron* case centered on the controversial "bubble concept."[3] The 1977 amendments to the Clean Air Act (CAA) required states that had failed to reach national air quality standards to institute a permitting program to facilitate a decrease in air pollution emissions from "any new or modified major stationary sources."[4] The term "stationary sources" was not defined by the CAA. In 1981, the Environmental Protection Agency (EPA) promulgated a regulation that allowed states to adopt the "bubble concept" or "plantwide" concept of "stationary sources" under their permit programs.[5] Such an interpretation calculated plant emissions as a whole, rather than calculating emission from each individual pollution-emitting device. Therefore, a plant, which often contained more than one source of air pollution, could increase emissions from one device as long as there was a corresponding decrease within the same "industrial grouping" or "bubble."[6] The Natural Resources Defense Council petitioned the U.S. Court of Appeals for the District of Columbia Circuit to set aside the regulation—arguing that such an interpretation of "stationary source" was contrary to the statute's purpose of improving air quality.[7] The D.C. Circuit set aside the regulation as contrary to the CAA and the case was appealed to the U.S. Supreme Court.[8]

The Supreme Court reversed the D.C. Circuit decision, finding the EPA regulation to be a permissible exercise of authority under the CAA.[9] In doing so, the unanimous[10] opinion, authored by Justice Stevens, laid out a basic two-part test to be applied in reviewing an agency's construction of its own statutory authority. In an oft-quoted passage, Justice Stevens summarized the test, which itself encapsulates the relationship between the courts, the agencies, and Congress in administering and interpreting statutes:

> First, always, is the question whether Congress has directly spoken to the precise question at issue. If the intent of Congress is clear, that is the end of the matter; for the court, as well as the agency, must give effect to the

> unambiguously expressed intent of Congress. If, however, the court determines Congress has not directly addressed the precise question at issue, the court does not simply impose its own construction on the statute, as would be necessary in the absence of an administrative interpretation. Rather if the statute is silent or ambiguous with respect to the specific issue, the question for the court is whether the agency's answer is based on a permissible construction of the statute.[11]

Stevens's *Chevron* analysis established what many commentators have considered to be a highly deferential judicial role when faced with a challenge to an agency's interpretation of its own authorizing statute or a statute it administers.[12] At step one, a reviewing court must determine whether Congress has spoken clearly on the issue at hand and give effect to any intent it finds Congress expressed unambiguously.[13] An agency interpretation that is contrary to the clear intent of Congress must be rejected. If, however, Congress's intent is unclear as to the immediate question, including where Congress is silent, at step two the court's role is to defer to any reasonable agency interpretation of the pertinent statutory language.[14] This analysis is commonly referred to as the *Chevron* "two-step."[15]

In applying the test, at step one Justice Stevens looked at both the statutory text of the CAA and the statute's legislative history to determine if Congress had clearly expressed a position on stationary sources or the bubble concept.[16] Finding no evidence that Congress had "directly spoken to the precise question at issue," Stevens moved to step two of the *Chevron* analysis and concluded that the EPA "plantwide" regulation was indeed a reasonable or "permissible" construction of the CAA.[17]

In support of his analytical framework, Justice Stevens identified three key rationales for according deference to an agency's statutory interpretation: congressional delegation, agency expertise, and political accountability. Under the congressional delegation rationale, once Congress delegates the authority to administer a program or statutory scheme to an agency, that delegation "necessarily requires the formulation of policy and the making of rules to fill any gap left, implicitly or explicitly, by Congress."[18] Thus, an agency's authority to fill "gaps" in the face of statutory uncertainty precludes a court from substituting its own judgment "for a reasonable interpretation made by the administrator of an agency."[19] Under *Chevron*, resolving statutory uncertainty by choosing between reasonable interpretations of statutory language represents a policy decision better answered by the agency that has been delegated policymaking authority by Congress than answered by a court.

Deference to an agency's interpretation is also appropriate out of respect for the agency's substantive expertise in the area addressed by the statute. As Justice Stevens noted in his opinion, "judges are not experts in the field" and difficult interpretive decisions often require more than just "ordinary knowledge respecting the matters subjected to agency regulations."[20]

Finally, Justice Stevens alluded to political accountability as a justification for granting deference to agency interpretations. Stevens noted that judges have no true constituency and are not accountable to the public for their decisions, and therefore should not substitute their interpretation of an ambiguous statute for the reasonable interpretation of an agency.[21] "While agencies are not directly accountable to the people," wrote Justice Stevens, "the Chief Executive is, and it is entirely appropriate for this political branch of the government to make such policy choices—resolving the competing interests which Congress itself either inadvertently did not resolve, or intentionally left to be resolved by the agency charged with the administration of the statute in light of everyday realities."[22]

THE *CHEVRON* LEGACY

The legal framework laid out in *Chevron* by Justice Stevens has been cited in over 11,000 judicial opinions,[23] and yet at the time, Stevens felt that his opinion was much closer to a simple restatement of the law than a groundbreaking precedent.[24] As *Chevron* became regarded as a fundamental statement in administrative law, however, consistency in its application proved elusive. Questions about when and how to apply the *Chevron* analysis remain unsettled.

Authority and Influence

The *Chevron* decision has governed the balance of power between agencies and the courts in interpreting statutes for over 25 years. Although many commentators have argued that the case's authority has dwindled in recent years, the opinion continues to be cited with regularity, and while the *Chevron* test continues to evolve, the basic Stevens framework continues to be looked to as an authority in delineating the different interpretive roles of courts and agencies.

Though not always controlling, Justice Stevens's opinion in *Chevron* is triggered anytime an agency formally, or otherwise with the "force of law," interprets its authorizing statute or a statute that it administers.[25] Therefore, anytime an agency attempts to formally clarify a statutory ambiguity in the course of implementing a law and that interpretation is subsequently challenged, a court will most likely consider, if not apply, the *Chevron* framework.[26] Agencies often use these statutory clarifications as justifications for significant agency action that some might see as inappropriately diminishing or expanding a statute's intended impact. Accordingly, the opinion has played a large role in a number of landmark cases on alleged agency overreaching in derogation of the will of Congress. For example, the Court invoked *Chevron* in striking down the Food and Drug Administration's early attempts to exercise regulatory authority over tobacco products in *FDA v. Brown & Williamson Tobacco*.[27]

Still, *Chevron*'s influence is arguably waning.[28] A number of commentators have suggested that the Court has less frequently turned to *Chevron* as its basis for a holding involving agency statutory interpretation—at times even ignoring the case in situations where it would have otherwise been applicable.[29] Concurrent with this decrease in the case's use as a controlling precedent, a series of Court opinions has expressly restricted the circumstances in which *Chevron* potentially applies.[30]

Inconsistent Application and Unresolved Questions

As much as Justice Stevens's opinion has been cited, major questions remain about when and how to properly apply the *Chevron* test. The threshold question of what agency interpretations qualify for *Chevron* deference, for example, remains unclear. A second ongoing dispute, and one in which Justice Stevens has played a leading role, relates to what tools of statutory construction are properly employed at step one of the test as a court determines Congress's "intent." Specifically, should the court be considering legislative intent and legislative purpose or restrict itself to the statutory language alone?

A 2009 Supreme Court case entitled *Entergy Corp. v. Riverkeeper, Inc.* provides a clearly visible example of the degree of confusion associated with the application of the *Chevron* test.[31] More than 20 years after the *Chevron* decision—and after thousands of judicial citations—the Supreme Court is still arguing over even the most basic aspect of the *Chevron* test: which step must come first? In *Entergy*, the majority upheld an interpretation by EPA of "best technology available" that included a consideration of the technology's cost.[32]

Justice Scalia, writing for the majority, began his analysis by determining that EPA's position was a "reasonable interpretation of the statute."[33] In dissent, Justice Stevens criticized the majority for applying the reasonableness test of step two before considering whether Congress had clearly spoken to the question at issue in step one.[34] Stevens characterized the majority opinion as "puzzling in light of the commonly understood practice that, as a first step, we ask 'whether Congress has directly spoken to the precise question at issue.'"[35] Stevens then accused the majority of "assuming ambiguity and moving to the second step."[36]

When Does Chevron Apply?: Step Zero

In 2001, the Supreme Court added a new threshold requirement, or "step zero," to the *Chevron* analysis.[37] In *U.S. v. Mead Corp.*, the Court confined *Chevron* deference to limited types of agency interpretations.[38] Writing for the majority, Justice Souter determined that "administrative implementation of a particular statutory provision qualifies for *Chevron* deference when it appears that *Congress delegated authority* to the agency generally to make rules carrying the *force of law*, and that the agency interpretation claiming deference was promulgated in the exercise of that authority."[39] Justice Stevens agreed with Justice Souter's "force of law" threshold limitation and joined the majority opinion.[40]

Mead, along with a case entitled *Christensen v. Harris*,[41] established that the applicability of *Chevron* deference would turn largely on the formality of the process through which the agency adopted its interpretation and the extent to which Congress had delegated authority to the agency. Policy statements, agency manuals, and interpretive letters, for example, do not warrant *Chevron*-level deference.[42] Formal rules and other interpretations holding the "force of law" promulgated pursuant to delegated authority, however, would qualify for *Chevron* deference.[43] The Court also suggested that those interpretations that failed to qualify for *Chevron* deference would still receive so called *Skidmore* deference.[44] Under *Skidmore v. Swift & Co.*, a court will defer to an agency interpretation to the extent that the interpretation is persuasive.[45]

The "force of law" standard from *Mead* has not been clearly articulated. In *Mead* itself, the majority noted the determination was not simply whether the interpretation was made via formal rulemaking, "for we have sometimes founds reasons for *Chevron* deference even when no such administrative formality was required and none was afforded."[46] To further obfuscate the threshold question, the Court has also added a number of factors to be considered in determining whether an interpretation qualifies for *Chevron* deference. In *Barnhart v. Walton*, the Court, with Justice Stevens's support, referenced the importance of "the interstitial nature of the legal question, the related expertise of the Agency, the importance of the question to administration of the statute, the complexity of that administration, and the careful consideration the agency has given the question over a long period of time."[47] Given the confusion associated with the *Mead* standard, Justice Scalia, who has opposed the additional threshold layer imposed by *Mead* and its progeny, has argued in dissent that the Court will be "sorting out the consequence of the *Mead* doctrine ... for years to come."[48]

Permissible Tools of Statutory Construction for Use at Step One

Justice Stevens has played a prominent role in another ongoing dispute over the application of the *Chevron* test. A clear "textualist-intentionalist divide" has emerged on the Court with respect to the investigation at step one as to whether Congress has spoken to the precise issue in question.[49] Justice Stevens has consistently expressed his intentionalist view that legislative history and legislative purpose play a prominent role in determining Congress's intent.[50] In a footnote in *Chevron*, for example, Justice Stevens stated that a reviewing court should employ "traditional tools of statutory construction."[51] Stevens then went on to consider the text, purpose, and legislative history of the CAA before concluding that the statute was ambiguous as to the precise meaning of "stationary source."[52]

Justice Scalia, on the other hand, has led the opposition to the use of legislative history and legislative purpose, pushing strongly for a purely textualist approach to discerning whether a statute is ambiguous.[53] Under Stevens's *Chevron* approach, the first step is to ask whether Congress's intent is clear, while under Scalia's *Chevron* approach, the first step is simply to ask whether the enacted text is clear. Although initially following the Stevens approach, the majority of the Court now seems to generally support Scalia's textualist position.[54] At least one commentator has asserted that "[t]oday, *Chevron*'s first step is routinely described and applied as a search for mere textual clarity."[55] Stevens, however, has continued to assert his intentionalist position in a string of concurrences and dissents.[56]

What is perhaps the best example of the Stevens-Scalia interpretive divide can be found in a 2007 case entitled *Zuni Public School District No. 89 v. Department of Education*.[57] In *Zuni*, the majority, invoking *Chevron*, upheld an interpretation by the Secretary of Education of the Impact Aid Act's "equalization requirement" for aid expenditures to public school districts.[58] The case presented an atypical situation where the legislative history behind the provision seemed to suggest a congressional understanding contrary to the plain language of the statute. In an opinion written by Justice Breyer, the majority initially seemed to favor the textualist approach, noting that "normally neither the legislative history nor the reasonableness of the Secretary's method would be determinative if the plain language of the statute unambiguously indicated that Congress sought to foreclose the Secretary's interpretation," but then turned to legislative history and purpose "because of the technical language of the language in question."[59] Based on an evaluation of the statute's history, the majority determined that Congress's intent was unclear, and that the agency's interpretation was reasonable.

Justice Stevens, though joining the court's ultimate conclusion, wrote a separate concurrence in which he underscored the importance of legislative history in the *Chevron* analysis. Relying on the "clarity" of the provision's legislative history, Stevens determined that the agency had given effect to Congress's clearly expressed intent.[60] Therefore, the inquiry could be resolved at step one of the *Chevron* test. In reaching his conclusion, Stevens cited *Chevron*'s proposition that the court must employ "traditional tools of statutory construction" in giving effect to Congress's intent.[61] "Analysis of legislative history," Stevens continued, "is, of course, a traditional tool of statutory construction. There is no reason why we must confine ourselves to, or begin analysis with, the statutory text if other tools of statutory construction provide better evidence of congressional intent with respect to the precise point at issue."[62] Given the statutory provision's legislative history, Stevens was willing to defer to evidence of Congress's intent over clear statutory text to the contrary.

In dissent, Justice Scalia's analysis, which was joined by Chief Justice Roberts and Justice Thomas, began and ended with the plain language of the statute. Finding the agency's interpretation to be contrary to the "crystal-clear text" of the statute, Justice Scalia did not feel the *Chevron* analysis should move beyond step one.[63] His dissent emphasized the importance of the statutory text, and repeatedly criticized Justice Stevens, as well as the majority opinion, for their reliance on legislative history. Scalia saw "no reason to resort to legislative history," noting that the "only sure indication of what Congress intended is what Congress enacted."[64]

CHEVRON'S FUTURE

As Justice Stevens retires, how the new Court resolves the ambiguities associated with applying the *Chevron* test will have a tremendous impact on *Chevron*'s ultimate legacy. A narrow construction of the threshold limitation for *Chevron* deference established in *Mead* will likely lead to fewer scenarios in which a court is willing to accord substantial deference to an agency's statutory interpretation. Additionally, the more the court limits itself to a pure textual interpretation at step one of the analysis, the less of a role legislative history and legislative purpose will play in discerning Congress's intentions. Specifically, a Court that strongly favors the Scalia textualist approach will give less credence to congressional reports, hearings, and floor statements in determining the purpose and limits of congressional delegations to agencies. Especially with respect to the intentionalist-textualist divide, the impending departure of Justice Stevens—the leader of the intentionalist camp—could have significant consequences for the future of the *Chevron* doctrine.

The legal framework laid out by Justice Stevens in his *Chevron* opinion is at once ubiquitous and nebulous. The case is one of the most cited of all time, and yet its proper application remains unsettled. As the Court prepares for the departure of the Justice who authored the *Chevron* test, the test itself will continue to play a role in balancing the interpretive roles of courts and administrative agencies for the foreseeable future.

End Notes

[1] Chevron U.S.A Inc. v. NRDC, 467 U.S. 837, 839 (1984).

[2] *Chevron* is reportedly the most frequently cited case in administrative law and currently the second most frequently cited case ever behind *Erie Railroad Co. v. Tompkins*, 304 U.S. 64 (1938). Thomas W. Merrill, *The Story of* Chevron*: The Making of an Accidental Landmark*, Administrative Law Stories 399 (Peter Strauss ed., 2006).

[3] *Chevron*, 467 U.S. at 839 (1984).

[4] 42 U.S.C. § 7502.

[5] 40 C.F.R. § 51.18.

[6] *Chevron*, 467 U.S. at 839.

[7] *Id.* at 841.

[8] NRDC v. Gorsuch, 685 F.2d 718 (D.C. Cir. 1982).

[9] *Chevron*, 467 U.S. at 845 ("EPA's use of [the bubble] concept here is a reasonable policy choice for the agency to make.").

[10] Only six justices took part in the decision. Justices Marshall, Rehnquist, and O'Connor did not participate.

[11] *Chevron*, 467 U.S. at 842-43.

[12] *See, e.g.* Cass Sunstein, *Law and Administration after* Chevron, 90 Colum. L. Rev. 2071, 2075 (1990) (calling *Chevron* a "counter-Marbury").

[13] *Chevron*, 467 U.S. at 843 fn.9 ("[T]hat intention is the law and must be given effect.").

[14] *Id.* at 843.

[15] Kathryn A. Watts, *From* Chevron *to* Massachusetts*: Justice Stevens's Approach to Securing the Public Interest*, 43 U.C. Davis L. Rev. 1021 (2010).

[16] *Chevron*, at 859-65.

[17] *Id.* at 865 ("In these cases the Administrators interpretation represents a reasonable accommodation of manifestly competing interests and is entitled to deference.").

[18] *Id.* at 843-44.

[19] *Id.* at 844.

[20] *Id.* at 865.

[21] *Id.*

[22] *Id.*

[23] According to a LexisNexis search conducted on May, 24, 2010, the Chevron case has been cited in 11,607 federal and state cases.

[24] Merrill, *supra* note 2, at 420 (describing Stevens's comments that the case was "routine" and a restatement of existing law.) *See also* Watts, *supra* note 15, at 9. Consistent with his view, in a 2009 case Stevens asserted that "[j]udicial deference to agencies' views on statutes they administer was not born in *Chevron*." Negusie v. Holder, 129 S. Ct. 1159, 1170 (2009).

[25] U.S. v. Mead Corp., 533 U.S. 218, 226-227 (2001).

[26] There are also times when the Court has simply ignored *Chevron*. *See, e.g.*, Brotherhood of Locomotive Engineers v. Atchison Topeka & Santa Fe Railroad Co., 516 U.S. 152 (ignoring *Chevron* in a case involving a Federal Railroad Administration interpretation of the Hours of Service Act).

[27] 529 U.S. 120 (2000).

[28] *See*, Linda Jellum, *Chevron's Demise: A Survey of Chevron from Infancy to Senescence*, 59 Admin. L. Rev. 725 (2007) (arguing that *Chevron*'s influence is narrowing).

[29] *Id.* at 772-81.

[30] *See, e.g.*, U.S. v. Mead Corp., 533 U.S. 218, 226-227 (2001); Jellum, *supra* note 28, at 772.

[31] 129 S.Ct 1498 (2009).

[32] *Id.* at 1510.

[33] *Id.* at 1505.

[34] *Id.* at 1518 n. 5 (Stevens, J., dissenting).

[35] *Id.*

[36] *Id.*

[37] Cass Sunstein, *Step Zero*, 92 Va. L. Rev. 187, 207 (2006).

[38] 533 U.S. 218 (2001).

[39] *Id.* at 226-227 (emphasis added).

[40] Perhaps surprisingly, Justice Stevens has not written a major opinion with respect to the *Mead* limitation. *See*, Amy J. Wildermuth, *Solving the Puzzle of* Mead *and* Christensen*: What Would Justice Stevens Do*? 74 Fordham L. Rev. 1877, 1900 (2006) ("Although Justice Stevens had never shied away from writing separately, he has not authored any of the majority opinions in this area and thus has never crafted the test.").

[41] 529 U.S. 576 (2000).

[42] *Id.* at 587.

[43] *Id.*; *Mead*, 533 U.S. at 220-28.

[44] *Mead*, 533 U.S. 221. The proper application of *Skidmore* deference, much like *Chevron* deference, remains up for debate. Wildermuth, *supra* note 40, at 1888.

[45] 323 U.S. 134 (1944).

[46] *Id.* at 231.

[47] 535 U.S. 212 (2002).

[48] *Id.* at 239 (Scalia, J., dissenting). Scalia's dissent also predicted "uncertainty, unpredictability, and endless litigation" as a result of the increased use of *Skidmore* deference in the face of the new *Mead* limitation on *Chevron*. *Id.* at 250.

[49] Jellum, *supra* note 28, at 728.

[50] *Id.* at 743-748 (discussing Stevens's intentionalist approach)

[51] *Id.* at 843 n. 9

[52] *Id.* at 851-864.

[53] *Id.* at 748-753 (discussing Scalia's textualist approach)

[54] *Id.* at 761.

[55] Jellum, *supra* note 28, at 761. *But see* Zuni Pub. Sch. Dist. No. 89 v. Dep't of Educ., 550 U.S. 81 (2007) (invoking legislative history). However, the broader investigation into legislative history has been used by some Justices in coming to a determination of "reasonableness" at step two of the *Chevron* test. Jellum, *supra* note 28, at 761-62.

[56] *See, e.g.*, Young v. Community Nutrition Institute, 476 U.S. 974 (1986) (Stevens, J., dissenting); MCI Telecomms. Corp. v. AT&T Co., 512 U.S. 218 (1994) (Stevens, J., dissenting); Rapanos v. U.S., 547 U.S. 715 (2006) (Stevens, J., dissenting); Zuni Pub. Sch. Dist. No. 89 v. Dep't of Educ., 550 U.S. 81 (2007) (Stevens, J., concurring); Entergy Corp. v. Riverkeeper, Inc., 128 S. Ct. 1498 (2009) (Stevens, J., dissenting).

[57] 550 U.S. 81 (2007)

[58] *Id.* at 84-6.

[59] *Id.* at 93, 90.

[60] *Id.* at 106 (Stevens, J., concurring) ("Given the clarity of the evidence of Congress' 'intention on the precise question at issue,' I would affirm.").

[61] *Id.* at 105.

[62] *Id.* at 106.

[63] *Id.* at 122 (Scalia, J., dissenting). "The plain language of the federal Impact Aid statute clearly and unambiguously forecloses [the Secretary's interpretation]. Her selection of that methodology is therefore entitled to zero deference under [*Chevron*]." *Id.* at 108.

[64] *Id.* at 122.

In: Jurisprudence of Supreme Court Justice... ISBN: 978-1-61761-282-4
Editor: Harvey B. Lymont

Chapter 8

THE JURISPRUDENCE OF JUSTICE JOHN PAUL STEVENS: LEADING OPINIONS ON THE FREE SPEECH CLAUSE OF THE FIRST AMENDMENT

Kathleen Ann Ruane

SUMMARY

Justice Stevens has authored a number of significant opinions expounding upon the constitutional right to freedom of speech. Among them are significant cases related to indecency and the rights of broadcasters ("Seven Dirty Words Case"), commercial speech, symbolic speech, and the freedom of association. This chapter will describe these cases with a view to their impact on free speech case law, and their continuing relevance in the future. This chapter will not discuss Justice Stevens's election law-related opinions.

INTRODUCTION

Justice Stevens has authored a number of important majority opinions and dissents expounding upon the limits of the Free Speech Clause of the First Amendment. Justice Stevens is not a free speech absolutist. His opinions have been guided by an apparent desire to allow the government to impose reasonable restrictions on speech, while scrutinizing, particularly closely, instances in which the government bans specific modes of expression entirely.

The primary areas in which Justice Stevens has authored controlling decisions are regulation of indecency over broadcast and the Internet, regulation of indecency in general, and commercial speech. Stevens has also authored important dissents in cases addressing the constitutionality of laws banning the burning of an American flag, and free association rights.

This chapter discusses Justice Stevens's opinions in these areas.[1]

SPEECH OVER RADIO AND TELEVISION BROADCAST

Perhaps the most famous free speech decision authored by Justice Stevens is *Federal Communications Commission v. Pacifica Foundation*.[2] This case has come to be known as the "Seven Dirty Words" case or the "Filthy Words" case. The case arose out of an adjudication the Federal Communications Commission (FCC) had undertaken against Pacifica Foundation for broadcasting a monologue by the comedian George Carlin at 2 o'clock in the afternoon. In the monologue, Carlin repeatedly used seven particularly inflammatory words that "you couldn't say on the public ... airwaves."[3] All parties agreed that the monologue was not obscene and did not fit the definition for obscenity. The case, thus, squarely presented to the court the question of whether the FCC could regulate speech over broadcast that is indecent, but is not obscene.

Justice Stevens took a methodical approach to the opinion, breaking down the issue presented into four separate questions: (1) the scope of the Court's review; (2) whether the FCC's order was a form of illegal censorship; (3) whether the broadcast was, in fact, indecent, under the applicable law; and (4) whether the order violated the First Amendment. After finding that the Court must focus its review on the FCC's determination that Carlin's monologue was indecent, and that the FCC's action was not illegal censorship, Stevens analyzed the more difficult questions presented by the case.

The statute being enforced by the FCC in this case was 18 U.S.C. § 1464 which forbids the utterance of "any obscene, indecent or profane language by means of radio communication." Justice Stevens observed that the statute is written in the disjunctive, implying that each word has a separate meaning. Despite the fact that 18 U.S.C. § 1461, containing similar language to ban "obscene, indecent, or profane" speech through the mail, had been construed by the Court to prohibit only obscene speech delivered through the mail, Stevens reasoned that Congress could not have intended the same standard to apply to different modes of delivering speech.

Furthermore, Stevens found that the accepted definition of indecency does not require an appeal to prurient interest. Rather, the term indecent "refers to nonconformance with accepted standards of morality." With that definition in mind, Justice Stevens had little trouble deciding that the "Filthy Words" broadcast was indecent.

The only question left for Justice Stevens to answer was whether restricting indecent speech over broadcast radio was constitutional under the First Amendment. Stevens concluded that it is. In making this determination, Justice Stevens paid particular attention to the unique nature of the broadcast medium when deciding that restricting indecent speech over broadcast stations did not violate the First Amendment.

Context for Justice Stevens, in this case and subsequent cases, was key. Even though the speech at issue was undisputedly "vulgar, "offensive," and "shocking," Stevens found that the monologue at issue in the case may have been protected speech in some contexts. Stevens went so far as to include a transcript of the monologue in its entirety as an appendix to the opinion. However, Justice Stevens wrote that, though the monologue may be protected in some contexts, it was not "entitled to absolute protection under all circumstances." Stevens set forth to analyze the context in which the speech occurred to determine whether the FCC's action was appropriate.

Justice Stevens went on to hold that restricting (but not banning) indecent speech over the broadcast airwaves is constitutional because (1) "the broadcast media have established a uniquely pervasive presence in the lives of all Americans" and (2) "broadcasting is uniquely accessible to children, even those too young to read."[4] Stevens seemed concerned by the unwilling listener happening upon this "vulgar" broadcast, perhaps as he was channel surfing for a station in his car. Stevens noted that a warning prior to the broadcast would not protect that unwilling listener. The hour of the broadcast (2 p.m.) also concerned Justice Stevens, because children were more likely to be listening at that hour. Stevens stressed that these factors weighed heavily in the Court's decision to uphold the FCC's action, and that the Court was not endorsing a broad indecency ban. Stevens made clear that a host of variables would continue to be important to constitutionally restricting indecent speech including time of day, the medium of delivery, and the content of the program.

This opinion is widely cited and remains precedent for many decisions related to speech over the broadcast airwaves.

Stevens's conviction that the broadcast medium is special carried over into his dissent in *FCC v. League of Women Voters*.[5] In that case, Justice Stevens would have voted to uphold a statute that banned broadcast stations that received public funds from editorializing. Stevens expressed concern for the unseen influence of government funding upon the editorial opinions of stations that receive the funds. In his estimation, it was a legitimate concern for Congress to address. Furthermore, he noted that broadcasting was unique in that it is the only mode of mass communication that requires a license from the federal government. In his view, the proper course would have been to uphold Congress's attempt to prevent some non-commercial broadcast stations, whose license to operate and funding depend upon the federal government, from potentially becoming propaganda purveyors should the government choose to pressure those stations to broadcast the government's view as the station's own in an editorial.

Online Speech

Consistent with the philosophy exhibited in the broadcast cases that context and form of speech factors heavily in the government's ability to restrict speech, Justice Stevens authored the opinion for the majority of the Court in *Reno v. American Civil Liberties Union*.[6] The case struck down for violating the First Amendment two provisions of the Communications Decency Act (CDA) that prohibited indecent speech to minors on the Internet. Stevens wrote that the "burden on adult speech is unacceptable if less restrictive alternatives would be at least as effective in achieving the legitimate purpose that the statute was enacted to serve," making clear that a higher standard of scrutiny would apply to restrictions of speech on the Internet than restrictions of speech over broadcast. Stevens continued: "[T]he governmental interest in protecting children from harmful materials ... does not justify an unnecessarily broad suppression of speech addressed to adults. As we have explained, the Government may not 'reduc[e] the adult population ... to ... only what is fit for children.'"[7]

In distinguishing between the Internet and other forms of mass communication, Stevens found that "[t]he CDA's broad categorical prohibitions are not limited to particular times and are not dependent on any evaluation by an agency familiar with the unique characteristics of the Internet." Thus the restrictions on indecent speech over broadcast media were more narrowly tailored than the speech restriction in this case. Furthermore, Stevens took issue with the fact that the CDA imposed criminal penalties, and the Court has never decided whether indecent broadcasts "would justify a criminal prosecution." Lastly, in Steven's estimation, radio and television, unlike the Internet, have, "as a matter of history ... received the most limited First Amendment protection ... in large part because warnings could not adequately protect the listener from unexpected program content.... [On the Internet], the risk of encountering indecent material by accident is remote because a series of affirmative steps is required to access specific material."

Justice Stevens dissented from the Court's decision in *United States v. American Library Association*, which upheld provisions of the Children's Internet Protection Act (CIPA) prohibiting the receipt of federal assistance for Internet access by public libraries that failed to install software to filter pornographic images.[8] Justice Stevens argued that the provision mandated, paradoxically, "underblocking" and "overblocking" of websites. Technology, at the time, could only filter text on a web page; therefore, if a website contained only indecent or pornographic images, the filtering software would not block it. This was Justice Stevens's reason for finding an "underblocking" problem. The "overblocking" issue also arose out of the software's heavy reliance on words, because words chosen for blocking could be pornographic in one context, but scientific, educational, or innocuous in another. Stevens explained, "[in] my judgment, a statutory blunderbuss that mandates this vast amount of 'overblocking' abridges the freedom of speech protected by the First Amendment." Stevens was also troubled by the fact that if even one computer with Internet access in a public library was not equipped with the filtering software, regardless of whether that computer was funded in part by federal assistance, the public library would be ineligible for federal funds.

SECONDARY EFFECTS AND ADULT ESTABLISHMENTS

Justice Stevens exhibited his belief that government attempts to ban particular types of content require more exacting scrutiny in the opinions that he wrote related to regulation of adult establishments. In *Young v. American Mini-Theaters, Inc.*, Stevens authored the opinion for the Court upholding a local ordinance requiring movie theaters that predominantly exhibit adult movies to be a certain distance away from one another.[9] Stevens noted that even when speech is protected, differences in content may permit different government responses. In this case, with recognition that adult establishments are associated with urban blight, lower property values, and other unsavory effects on neighborhoods, Stevens found that the government "may legitimately use the content of these materials as the basis for placing them in a different classification than other movie theaters," under the Equal Protection Clause of the Fourteenth Amendment. However, Stevens emphasized that this was not a complete ban on these establishments, nor was it a restriction on what types of content these establishments could display. Rather, the restriction was "nothing more than a limitation on the place where adult films may be exhibited," and was therefore constitutional.

Justice Stevens dissented, however, from the Court's decision to uphold a city ordinance that required women in adult dance clubs to wear pasties and a G-string, thereby preventing them from dancing completely naked. [10] The case was *City of Erie v. Pap's A.M., TDBA "Kandyland."* Stevens distinguished this case from his holding in *Young*.[11] First, the ordinance in *Young* did not burden the content of the speech at issue; here, a particular type of content (dancing naked) would be banned entirely. Furthermore, in *Young* the ordinance attempted to manage the secondary effects of these establishments by spreading them out. In this case, in Stevens's opinion, there seemed to be no reason to believe that requiring dancers to wear pasties and a G-string would reduce the tendency of the establishments to attract crime and prostitution. Stevens argued that this ordinance did not seek to reduce secondary effect of adult establishments, and, instead, did nothing more than entirely ban a mode of protected expression.

COMMERCIAL SPEECH

Justice Stevens has written a number of opinions furthering the Court's jurisprudence regarding First Amendment protections for commercial speech. Repeatedly, Stevens has made clear that commercial speech restrictions that ban particular types of truthful content deserve more exacting scrutiny and are constitutionally suspicious. In *44 Liquormart, Inc. v. Rhode Island*, Justice Stevens, writing for the majority, invalidated a statute that prohibited alcohol price advertisements.[12] In doing so, Justice Stevens made clear that a total prohibition on "the dissemination of truthful, nonmisleading commercial messages for reasons unrelated to the preservation of a fair bargaining process" will be subject to a stricter review by the courts than a regulation designed "to protect consumers from misleading, deceptive, or aggressive sales practices." Stevens added, "[the] First Amendment directs us to be especially skeptical of regulations that seek to keep people in the dark for what the government perceives to be their own good." Many viewed this decision as increasing the constitutional protection for truthful and nonmisleading commercial speech.

Stevens also authored the opinion in *City of Cincinnati v. Discovery Network*.[13] That case made clear that commercial speech restrictions are, in fact, content based restrictions on speech, and that restrictions on commercial speech should relate to the interests the government seeks to advance. [14] In this case, the city had enacted a ban on news racks that contained commercial publications. Its reasons for enacting the ban were primarily aesthetic; however, the ban did not apply to newspapers or other publications that were not "primarily commercial" in nature. This fact led Justice Stevens to observe that "[not] only does Cincinnati's categorical ban on commercial news racks place too much importance on the distinction between commercial and noncommercial speech, but in this case, the distinction bears no relationship *whatsoever* to the particular interests that the city has asserted."[15] Stevens conceded that there may be instances wherein a government could assert permissible reasons for distinguishing between commercial and noncommercial news racks, but that the city had failed to do so in this case.

In *Greater New Orleans Broadcasting Ass 'n v. United States*, Justice Stevens invalidated a ban on casino advertising over broadcast stations located in states where gambling was legal.[16] Stevens rejected the "greater includes the lesser" argument previously adopted by the Court in *Posadas de Puerto Rico Associations v. Tourism Co. of P.R.*, 478 U.S. 328 (1986). Justice Stevens made clear that simply because government could ban the underlying activity all together (gambling), that did not mean government could ban advertising or other forms of speech about that activity. Furthermore, Stevens found that, even in a commercial speech context, there is presumption that "the speaker and the audience, not the government, should be left to assess the value of accurate and nonmisleading information about lawful conduct."[17] Consistent with this opinion, Justice Stevens dissented from the earlier case, *United States v. Edge Broadcasting*, which upheld the statute at issue in *Greater New Orleans Broadcasting*, when it was applied to broadcast stations located in states that forbid gambling that were seeking to broadcast advertisements for gambling establishments in states where gambling was legal.[18] Stevens wrote "the United States has selected the most intrusive, and dangerous form of regulation possible—a ban on truthful information regarding a lawful activity imposed for the purpose of manipulating, through ignorance, the consumer choices of some of its citizens. Unless justified by a truly substantial governmental interest, this extreme, and extremely paternalistic, measure surely cannot withstand scrutiny under the First Amendment."[19]

SYMBOLIC SPEECH

Justice Stevens authored a brief dissent from the Court's decision in *Texas v. Johnson*. In that case, the Court overturned a criminal conviction for desecration of the American flag. Stevens emphasized the importance of the American flag as a unique symbol of "the courage, the determination, and the gifts of nature that transformed" the United States into a world power. Stevens argued that a law that prohibited desecration of that symbol would not suppress the message that was attempting to be conveyed by the act of desecration. Rather, Stevens argued the law prohibited "disagreeable conduct." Stevens would have upheld the conviction and the statute at issue. Stevens reasoned that no one would question a law prohibiting the desecration of the Lincoln Memorial. According to this logic, the "prohibition [on desecration of the Lincoln Memorial] would be supported by the legitimate interest in preserving the quality of an important national asset. Though the asset at stake in this case is intangible, given its unique value, the same interest supports a prohibition on the desecration of the American flag."[20]

BUFFER ZONES

Again exhibiting his willingness to uphold laws that reasonably restrict the time, place, or manner of speech, and a concomitant tendency to strike down laws that ban a particular form of expression in its entirety, Stevens wrote the opinion for the Court in a case that upheld certain restrictions on protesting near hospitals and medical facilities and authored the primary dissent from a case that upheld a ban on protesting specific residences. In *Hill v. Colorado*, the Court upheld the constitutionality of a statute that required protesters outside health care facilities to remain eight feet away from persons entering or exiting those facilities, unless they consented to the approach of the protesters.[21] Stevens began his opinion by noting that, contrary to the arguments of those opposed to the law, the law was content neutral. The question of content neutrality, particularly in cases that involve time, place, and manner restrictions, "is whether the government has adopted a regulation of speech because of disagreement with the message conveyed."[22] Stevens made clear that the restriction at issue here was not a "regulation of speech." Rather it was "a regulation of the places where some speech may occur." Furthermore, the law restricted all protesters outside of health care facilities regardless of viewpoint, lending further support to the finding that it was content neutral. Stevens, therefore, applied the relevant constitutional test for content neutral time, place, and matter restrictions on speech. Stevens found that the law was a valid and narrowly tailored government effort to balance the interests of protesters against the privacy interests of those entering and exiting health care facilities, who may find themselves in a particularly vulnerable position. He noted that the eight foot restriction is close enough that the protesters' message can be conveyed through speech, signs, etc., but preserves the personal space of those entering the facility. Also factoring in to Stevens's finding that the law was narrowly tailored was that the protesters could approach with the consent of the person they were attempting to counsel and that the eight foot restriction was only in effect within 100 feet of health care facilities. In Stevens's reasoning, this left open many alternative channels of communication and banned no one from engaging in constitutionally protected speech.

Consistent with his aversion to complete bans on speech, Justice Stevens dissented from the Court's decision to uphold a ban on protesting in front of single family homes in an earlier case, *Frisby v. Schultz*.[23] Stevens argued that it was "perfectly clear that the town could prohibit pedestrians from loitering in front of a residence. On the other hand, it [seemed] equally clear that a sign carrier [had] a right to march past a resident—and presumably pause long enough to give the occupants an opportunity to read [it]."[24] Stevens left open the possibility that he would support restrictions on picketing in front of residences if the ordinance was limited to conduct particularly intrusive to the privacy of the home.

FREEDOM OF ASSOCIATION

Justice Stevens authored the dissent for himself and three other Justices in *Boy Scouts of America v. Dale*.[25] The majority upheld the right of Boy Scouts of America (BSA) to exclude gay men from the organization, despite a New Jersey statute that prohibited discrimination on the basis of sexual orientation (among other characteristics, such as race and gender). The majority found that the statute violated BSA's First Amendment rights to freedom of speech and association.

Justice Stevens disagreed. First, Stevens noted that nothing in the BSA's bylaws or code of conduct prohibited homosexuality, and, to the extent that sex or sexual orientation was a topic in those documents, they expressly directed scouts and scout masters to seek counseling on those matters from parents or clergy, because it was not the primary mission of BSA. Then, citing cases in which the Court upheld a state's requirement that private, previously all-male clubs admit women, Stevens argued that the right to freely associate is not absolute. "The relevant question is whether the mere inclusion of the person at issue would 'impose any serious burden,' 'affect in any significant way,' or be a substantial restraint upon' the organization's 'shared goals, basic goals, or 'collective effort to foster beliefs.'"[26] Stevens could find no evidence that forbidding BSA from excluding homosexuals in its group would alter or burden any message expressed by BSA. Stevens returned to the inconsistency and lack of clarity in BSA's speech about homosexuals, and noted that if the organization is unclear in its expression, it is difficult then to conclude that an anti-discrimination law is a "serious burden."

Furthermore, Stevens argued that the inclusion of openly gay men in BSA likely would not force BSA to adopt or include a message with which it does not agree. Stevens distinguished the case from *Hurley v. Irish-American Gay, Lesbian, and Bisexual Group of Boston*, in which the Court refused to require a group holding a privately operated parade to include an openly gay group.[27] Stevens focused on the fact that the openly gay group would have been conveying a message by marching in the parade and that it was likely that their message would also be perceived as the message of the parade organizers. In contrast, the plaintiff in this case did not appear to be seeking to convey any message, and it seemed unlikely to Stevens that BSA would be seen by others as approving of every idea or expression held by each and every one of its members.

Therefore, Stevens, and the other dissenters, would have upheld New Jersey's anti-discrimination law and required BSA to include homosexuals as members.

Conclusion

In general, Justice Stevens appears to have consistently demonstrated a resistance to government speech restrictions that would effectively ban a particular type of speech or a particular avenue of conveying a message. However, Stevens upheld reasonable governmental restrictions on speech that did not have the effect of banning speech entirely. Stevens appeared to favor laws that channeled speech to more appropriate times, or more appropriate places, so long as the restrictions were reasonable. This approach is pragmatic. It appears to recognize the government interests in protecting its citizens from speech that could be offensive to some (indecency) or could have a particular tendency to mislead (commercial speech) while protecting the rights of people to communicate constitutionally protected speech.

End Notes

[1] This report will not discuss Justice Stevens's opinions in the areas of election law or campaign finance law.
[2] 438 U.S. 726 (1978).
[3] *Id.* at 729.
[4] *Id.* at 748-750.
[5] 468 U.S. 364 (1984).
[6] 521 U.S. 844 (1997).
[7] *Id.* at 874-75.
[8] 593 U.S. 194, 220 (2003) (Stevens, J. dissenting).
[9] 427 U.S. 50 (1976).
[10] 529 U.S. 277 (2000).
[11] *Id.* at 317.
[12] 517 U.S. 484 (1996).
[13] 507 U.S 410 (1993).
[14] This was the primary reason for refusing to uphold the statute at issue as a time, place, and manner restriction. *Id.* at 428-430.
[15] *Id.* at 424 (emphasis in original).
[16] 527 U.S. 173 (1999).
[17] *Id.* at 195.
[18] 509 U.S. 418 (1993).
[19] *Id.* at 439 (Stevens, J. dissenting).
[20] *Id.*

[21] 530 U.S. 703 (2000).
[22] *Id.* at 719 (quoting Ward v. Rock Against Racism, 491 U.S. 781, 791 (1989)).
[23] 487 U.S. 474, 496 (1988) (Stevens, J. dissenting).
[24] *Id.* at 497.
[25] 530 U.S. 640, 663 (2000) (Stevens, J. dissenting).
[26] *Id.* at 683.
[27] *Id.* at 590 (citing Hurley v. Irish-American Gay, Lesbian, and Bisexual Group of Boston, 515 U.S. 557, 568-570 (1995)).

CHAPTER SOURCES

The following chapters have been previously published:

Chapter 1 – This is an edited, reformatted and augmented version of a Congressional Research Service publication, report R41244, dated May 19, 2010

Chapter 2 - This is an edited, reformatted and augmented version of a Congressional Research Service publication, report R41246, dated May 18, 2010

Chapter 3 – This is an edited, reformatted and augmented version of a Congressional Research Service publication, report R41236, dated May 14, 2010

Chapter 4 – This is an edited, reformatted and augmented version of a Congressional Research Service publication, report R41238, dated May 13, 2010

Chapter 5 - This is an edited, reformatted and augmented version of a Congressional Research Service publication, report R41229, dated May 7, 2010

Chapter 6 – This is an edited, reformatted and augmented version of a Congressional Research Service publication, report R41276, dated June 7, 2010

Chapter 7 – This is an edited, reformatted and augmented version of a Congressional Research Service publication, report R41260, dated May 26, 2010

Chapter 8 - This is an edited, reformatted and augmented version of a Congressional Research Service publication, report R41256, dated May 27, 2010

INDEX

A

B

C

D

E

F

G

H

I

J

K

L

M

N

O

P

Q

R

W